CAREER CHOICE AND REALIGNMENT

A CAREER COMPANION FOR STUDENTS AND PROFESSIONALS

DEGREES OF CONFUSION,
WHY STUDENTS AND PROFESSIONALS
SWITCH PATH

VIJAY VASUDEVAN

ISBN
Hardcase 979-8-89929-931-5
Paperback 979-8-89929-353-5

Dedication

To every student wondering which path to choose.

To every professional questioning whether to stay or move on.

To the mentors who guide quietly, and the experiences that teach loudly.

And to my family—your unwavering belief in me made all things possible.

Are you choosing your career – or simply following one?

In *Career Choice and Realignment*, discover a powerful roadmap for students stepping into the unknown, professionals navigating mid-career dilemmas, and anyone seeking a meaningful shift in their journey. Drawing from decades of real-world experience across business, strategy, technology, and leadership, this book blends honest storytelling with practical insights. Whether you're choosing your first job, growing in your role, or contemplating a pivot, this guide helps you make intentional choices—backed by clarity, courage, and confidence.

Because the best careers aren't found. They're built—with purpose and realignment.

CONTENTS

Contents

PART V – For Mentors, Educators & Parents

PART VI – The Ultimate Career Compass

GUIDING PRINCIPLE FROM BHAVAD GEETHA FOR THIS BOOK

श्रेयान्स्वधर्मो विगुणः परधर्मात्स्वनुष्ठितात्‌।
स्वधर्मे निधनं श्रेयः परधर्मो भयावहः॥

– Bhagavad Gita – Chapter 3, Verse 35

Transliteration:

"Shreyān svadharmo viguṇaḥ paradharmāt svanuṣṭhitāt
Svadharme nidhanam śreyaḥ paradharmo bhayāvahaḥ"

Meaning:

"It is far better to perform one's own duty, even imperfectly, than to perform another's duty perfectly. Death in the path of one's own dharma (duty) is better; the duty of another is fraught with fear and danger."

Interpretation (in context of career choice and realignment):

This verse is a timeless piece of wisdom for **students, professionals, and seekers at any stage of life**. It tells us that **one's own chosen path**, even if filled with challenges or executed with flaws, is more meaningful than walking a path that doesn't align with your nature, just because it appears more successful or glamorous.

In terms of **career**, this shloka urges you to:

- Understand your **core strengths, interests, and inclinations** (your *svadharma*)
- Avoid blindly following others' choices (like picking a profession due to societal pressure)
- Embrace your own path—even if it has initial struggles—because **purpose is more powerful than prestige**

ACKNOWLEDGMENTS

Writing *Career Choice and Realignment* has been a journey of reflection, gratitude, and purpose. This book is not just a collection of thoughts but a culmination of years of learning, transitions, failures, and milestones.

I would like to extend my heartfelt thanks to all the leaders, peers, and teams I've worked with across organizations. Your collaboration and challenges shaped my perspectives and helped me grow.

A special thanks to Mr. Arun Diaz—your mentorship, insight, and compassion during my leadership journey left an indelible mark. Your approachability and vision inspired not just direction, but conviction.

To my family—thank you for being my grounding force. Your love and support have been the greatest strength behind all my professional endeavors.

And finally, to every reader picking up this book—thank you for trusting me with your time. I hope these pages bring clarity, courage, and the conviction to choose not just a career, but a calling.

PREFACE

As I sit down to write this book, I find myself reflecting on a journey that was neither pre-planned nor traditionally linear. It wasn't carved out by design but discovered through detours—through choices made in uncertainty, through dreams that had to be parked, and through passions that evolved with time. This book is a result of that journey—a humble offering for students, parents, professionals, and educators who are at the crossroads of career decision-making, searching for direction, purpose, and clarity.

I was never the class topper. In fact, I was a backbencher during my school years—an average student by most academic standards. My educational background was modest, and I had no elite degrees or dream career plans at the time. What I did have, however, was curiosity, sincerity, and a strong desire to serve my country. During my early college years, I served in the **National Cadet Corps (NCC)** and rose to the rank of **Senior Under Officer**. My performance, especially in **sharpshooting**, earned me accolades and, eventually, an opportunity to join the **Indian Defence Academy (IDA)**. I was prepared, determined, and driven to take that path.

But life had other plans. Despite my passion and preparation, I was emotionally restrained from pursuing that dream. My parents, concerned for my safety and swayed by societal expectations, denied me permission to join the forces. I was devastated. That moment became my first major **crossroad**—one where the heart's desire had to yield to family priorities.

In search of an alternative, I turned to something I was naturally drawn to—**computer programming**. I took up part-time coding classes and quickly discovered an aptitude for it. I loved the logic, the creativity, and the problem-solving aspects of coding. Yet again, fate had other plans. My elder brother, already working in the financial sector, helped me secure a job in an **NBFC (Non-Banking Financial Company)**. It wasn't a conscious career choice—it was a job to get started with. But once I stepped into that world, I chose to give it my all.

What followed was an uncharted, yet deeply enriching journey—from **Sales** to **Credit**, from **Collections** to **Audit**, from **Strategy** to **Business Transformation**, and finally to **Technology and IT Leadership**. Today, I served as a **Chief Information Officer (CIO) in NBFC and a Bank and Now Heading Business Transformation in a Bank**, having led large-scale digital transformation projects in banking and financial services. At the age of 38, I polished my technical foundation by completing the **Master CIO Certification at Carnegie Mellon University, USA**—an experience that blended my years of business experience with formal learning in cutting-edge technology and leadership.

The beauty of my journey lies in its imperfections. I wasn't the "ideal" student. I didn't pursue a linear career path. I didn't study at the world's top colleges in my early years. Yet, I built my career from the ground up—one role at a time, one lesson at a time. Every step taught me something valuable. I failed, I adapted, I evolved. And today, I use that lived experience to design technology that truly serves its users—internal employees, customers, field staff, or partners—because I understand what they need, having once been in their shoes.

I wrote this book because I've seen countless individuals—especially young students—waste valuable time and money pursuing careers they don't resonate with, simply because they were poorly guided or lacked exposure. I've seen brilliant minds give up too soon or go in circles because they didn't get the right advice at the right time. I wanted to write something **real**, **practical**, and **inspiring**—a guide that could help people navigate the confusing maze of career choices with clarity and courage.

This book is not about "success" in the conventional sense. It is about **alignment**—choosing a path that fits your skills, your temperament, your aspirations, and your evolving worldview. It is about understanding that **career is not a race, but a journey of discovery**—and the earlier you discover what aligns with you, the better equipped you are to reach your goals faster, and more meaningfully.

Though my career has been rooted in **banking and financial services**, the principles shared in this book apply across domains— be it **Pharma, Manufacturing, Trading, IT, Education**, or **Service industries**. I've built systems for frontline staff, decision-makers, and customers; I've seen how career misalignment creates dissatisfaction and how the right choices create lasting fulfillment. I've lived the business, learned the technology, and now, I'm writing to bridge the gap—for the next generation of professionals and parents shaping them.

Whether you're a student making your first big choice, a parent guiding your child, a professional rethinking your path, or a leader mentoring your team—this book is for you. I've distilled everything I've learned over **24+ years across functions and domains**, into actionable insights that can help you or someone you care about make better, faster, and more conscious career decisions.

Welcome to a journey of self-discovery, clarity, and courage.

– Vijay Vasudevan

PART I

FOUNDATIONS: THE EARLY CROSSROADS

Audience: Students (Class 8–12), Parents

Introduction: Where the Journey Truly Begins

Every great journey has a beginning—not always a grand or dramatic one, but often a quiet, uncertain step into the unknown. For most students, the first whispers of a career begin not in college or after graduation, but much earlier—sometimes as early as Class 6 or 7—when a teacher compliments them on a drawing, a parent remarks on their math ability, or a relative casually asks, "So, what do you want to be when you grow up?"

This first part of the book, Foundations: The Early Crossroads, explores that delicate, powerful phase of discovery when students begin navigating the complex world of future possibilities. It is the stage where impressions are formed, choices begin to crystallize, and the first seeds of identity are sown. Yet, it is also the most vulnerable time—when decisions are influenced by peer pressure, societal norms, and incomplete information. This section addresses those pivotal early years with empathy, insight, and practical wisdom.

We begin with "The Early Crossroads – Students and Their Initial Vocational Choices," which looks at how children and adolescents start forming ideas about careers—ideas that are often shaped not by deep understanding or passion but by exposure and expectation. In many cases, choices are made reactively—driven by what friends are doing, what's trending, or what seems 'safe'. This chapter highlights how important it is to create an environment where students can explore, ask questions, and gain real insight into different professions before being funneled into fixed academic streams.

The next chapter, "The Role of Parents in Career Decision-Making," emphasizes the massive influence parents have—both knowingly and unknowingly. In the Indian context, parents often play the role of decision-makers, not just influencers. Their intentions are rooted in care and security, but sometimes they unknowingly project their aspirations or fears onto their children. This chapter invites parents to become guides instead of directors—to listen more than instruct, to observe more than dictate. It urges families to create safe spaces for open conversations around career choices and to recognize that success comes in many forms, not just in conventional professions.

In "Understanding Strengths, Not Just Subjects," we dismantle the myth that academic excellence alone is a predictor of future success. Many students are led to believe that excelling in certain subjects automatically determines their career path—good in biology, become a doctor; good in math, become an engineer. But real-world success is far more complex. This chapter introduces the idea of identifying a child's core strengths—creativity, empathy, problem-solving, leadership, perseverance—and how those traits can be better indicators of suitable and fulfilling careers. It's about shifting the lens from *what* a child scores well in to *who* the child truly is.

The fourth chapter, "The Myth of the 'Only One Path,'" questions the dominant belief that only a handful of career paths are respectable or secure. For decades, Indian society has placed a disproportionate premium on engineering, medicine, and government jobs—often overlooking the rich array of meaningful and viable career options in the arts, entrepreneurship, design, sports, technology, and beyond. This chapter explores how dangerous it is to force-fit all students into the same molds and how we must start embracing diverse aspirations without judgment. It challenges the fear-driven mindset and makes a compelling case for exploring non-linear, non-traditional paths that align with evolving industries and global opportunities.

Finally, "Identifying Natural Strengths Early" ties it all together. It discusses the value of early aptitude assessments, observing behavioral cues, recognizing learning styles, and the critical role of mentorship. The earlier we identify what a child is naturally drawn toward or good at, the more time they have to develop mastery and confidence. This chapter also introduces tools and techniques—both formal and informal—that can help students discover their unique blend of talents and inclinations. Importantly, it outlines how parents, teachers, and counselors can collaborate in this process—not to rush a child toward a decision but to support a journey of exploration.

Together, these five chapters lay the foundation for meaningful career alignment. They call for a cultural shift—from seeing career choice as a one-time decision to recognizing it as a journey of discovery, self-awareness, and guided support. At the heart of this section is a simple yet transformative belief: Every child is born with potential. Our job is not to define it but to help uncover it.

As you read through these chapters, whether you are a parent, educator, or student, remember that the goal is not to find the perfect answer right away. The goal is to build a foundation where curiosity thrives, strengths are celebrated, and young minds are free to dream big—and dream true.

CHAPTER 1

The Early Crossroads – Students and Their Initial Vocational Choices

"You are not late. But you are also not too early to start asking the right questions."

1.1 Introduction: The Silent but Crucial Turning Point

The journey of life has many crossroads—but the first one often comes **quietly, without warning**, somewhere between 8th and 12th standard. It's not marked by dramatic signs. Instead, it shows up as simple, yet powerful questions:

- "Which stream should I choose?"
- "What should I become?"
- "Should I go with what I like or what earns more?"
- "What are my friends choosing?"

Most students either **ignore these questions** or answer them based on what their friends or parents say. The truth is—**this is the time when early awareness can create a lifetime of difference**.

Let's dive deep into what's happening in this stage of life—and how students and parents can make better decisions.

1.2 The Modern-Day Student: Living in a Labyrinth of Distractions

Imagine a student named *Gopi*, in 10th grade. His day starts with school, continues with coaching classes, but in between:

- He spends 2-3 hours a day on Instagram and YouTube.
- He plays mobile games late into the night.
- He binge-watches shows on weekends.
- He follows trends but doesn't follow his dreams.

Does this sound familiar?

The Reality:

Today's student is **surrounded by digital temptations**—not just distractions, but emotional hooks. Likes, followers, and gaming ranks give **instant dopamine hits**, but rarely bring clarity or growth.

These distractions are **not the enemy**, but **they take over when there's no purpose, no plan, and no passion guiding the student.**

1.3 Productivity vs. Activity: A Dangerous Misunderstanding

A lot of students feel "busy." They attend classes, they write exams, they do assignments. But ask them what they're working toward, and there's a blank stare.

What's Missing?

- **No personal goal beyond marks**
- **No structured time for self-learning**
- **No effort in building real-world skills**
- **No awareness about career paths outside of the 'usual ones'**

This is where the **difference between activity and productivity** must be taught. You can be active all day but not productive if you don't know what you're building.

1.4 The 'Marks-Only' Trap: A Narrow Lens on a Vast World

The majority of students and parents believe one dangerous idea:

"Higher marks = Better future."

But here's the reality:

- Some students with **average marks build amazing careers**.
- Many toppers are still **figuring out their paths in their late 20s**.
- **The world values problem-solvers**, not just exam-solvers.

Of course, marks matter. They open doors. But they don't **guarantee growth, joy, or satisfaction**. Early career discovery is far more powerful.

1.5 Lack of Guidance: Students Are Asking, "Whom Do I Ask?"

Most schools focus only on:

- Textbooks
- Board exams
- Entrance coaching

But no one sits down with students to ask:

- "What are you naturally good at?"
- "What do you enjoy doing in your free time?"
- "Have you spoken to someone working in that field?"
- "Have you tried an internship, a workshop, or a real-life project?"

When no one asks, students **stop thinking.**

Career guidance isn't a one-time seminar. It's a **continuous conversation**, which is unfortunately **missing in most homes and schools.**

1.6 Parental Influence: Love Mixed with Fear

Now, let's talk about parents.

Most parents want the best for their children. But their love is often wrapped in **fear and societal pressure**:

- "What if this field doesn't pay?"
- "My friend's son became a doctor—why not you?"
- "This passion of yours—can it get you a job?"
- "Arts? Are you serious?"

What Parents Often Miss:

- Today's job world is **changing fast**. There are new, high-potential domains in Data Science, Behavioral Economics, Green Technology, UI/UX Design, Sports, Psychology, Cybersecurity, etc.
- Career stability now comes from **multi-skilling, innovation, and adaptability**—not just job titles.
- Instead of pushing children toward safe zones, **they must be guided to future-ready spaces**.

1.7 The Peer Influence Dilemma: Everyone's Doing It, So Should I?

Students often choose streams not because they love them, but because:

- "My best friend took it."
- "Everyone in my tuition is going for IIT coaching."
- "Commerce is easy. Let's just go with that."

This kind of decision-making is like **blindfolded driving**—you may move forward, but with no idea where you're going.

Instead of choosing based on comfort or company, students must be encouraged to **choose based on calling**—even if it's an unconventional one.

1.8 Reflection Exercises: Let's Pause and Think

For Students:

1. What do I enjoy doing even when no one is watching or rewarding me?

2. What subject excites me more than the rest?

3. What job would I do for free if I had no pressure?

For Parents:

1. Am I listening to my child or just deciding for them?

2. Do I know what future careers are emerging today?

3. Can I give my child the space to explore, fail, and still support them?

1.9 A Better Way Forward: Awareness + Exposure + Mentorship

A new approach is needed. It involves:

- **Awareness**: Exposing students to different career options, industries, and stories.
- **Exploration**: Workshops, shadowing professionals, trying online courses.
- **Mentorship**: Connecting with industry professionals who can offer perspective.

This is how real-world career choices are made: not in isolation, but in **informed ecosystems**.

1.10 Conclusion: You Are at the Crossroads – Make It Count

This chapter is not meant to scare you—it's meant to **wake you up**.

If you're in 8th to 12th standard, this is the **golden phase**. Every hour you spend understanding yourself and the world of work will save **years of trial-and-error** later.

If you're a parent, this is your chance to become your child's greatest **coach**, not their controller.

Together, let's build a generation that is not just chasing jobs—but **building lives full of meaning, confidence, and direction.**

Chapter Summary: Key Messages

For Students	For Parents
Start early	Stay informed
Avoid distractions	Let go of fear
Don't follow blindly	Don't impose success formulas
Explore interests	Allow experimentation
Seek mentors	Encourage mentorships
Balance marks with skills	Balance expectations with empathy

CHAPTER 2

The Role of Parents in Career Decision-Making

"Behind every confident child choosing the right path is a parent who listened, learned, and let go at the right time."

2.1 Introduction: Parents – The First and Lasting Career Mentors

For every student standing at the edge of career choices between classes 8 to 12, one silent yet powerful influence often shapes the decision more than any teacher, counselor, or textbook—**their parents.**

Parents are not just providers of resources and support; they are often the **first career counselors** their children meet. The way a parent sees success, risk, education, or money—these silently guide the child's choices, fears, and dreams.

But not all guidance is conscious or helpful. Sometimes, **good intentions can unknowingly block the child's true potential.** Let's explore how parents can become enablers, not enforcers—and how the right involvement can make or break a child's career path.

2.2 Enabler vs. Enforcer: The Role Every Parent Must Reflect On

Many parents fall into the trap of **trying to shape their child's career** based on their own aspirations, missed opportunities, or societal pressure. Instead, the goal should be to **enable the child** to discover, explore, and own their interests.

An Enabler Parent:

- Listens more than instructs.
- Observes patterns of interest over time.
- Creates space for exploration.
- Invests time and money in enabling discovery.

An Enforcer Parent:

- Chooses the stream or career for the child.
- Sets goals based on prestige or peer comparison.
- Prioritizes marks over interest or talent.
- Focuses on stability and societal validation.

The goal is not to let children drift aimlessly, but to **guide them with patience, empathy, and flexibility.**

2.3 My Personal Journey with My Son, Sudharshan

Let me take a moment to share a **deeply personal story**—a journey of trial, error, observation, and eventual discovery with my son, **Sudharshan**.

As a parent, I was keen to understand what made him tick—what excited him, what kept him engaged. I started early. I **exposed him to a variety of activities**:

- **Football** – tried it, but lost interest.
- **Skating** – didn't connect with it.
- **Tennis** – same story.

Then I thought perhaps the creative side might be stronger. I tried introducing him to music:

- First came the **guitar** – he didn't find it appealing.
- Then came the **keyboard** – a bit better, but the spark still wasn't there.

Finally, I introduced him to **drums**—and this time, **something clicked.** He took to it with excitement and rhythm. He wasn't doing it for me or because it was popular. He was doing it because **he connected with it.**

- This journey taught me a powerful lesson:

"Interest and talent cannot be forced. They must be discovered."

Sometimes, **it's in the DNA.** You cannot expect a child to become an artist, a sportsperson, or a scientist if they are not wired for it. It's not about our ambition—it's about their nature.

Had I forced him into football or music just because I liked it, it would have ended in resistance or burnout. **Instead, I explored with him. I stood by him through the trial phases. I made time. I spent money. I observed. And finally, I saw him light up.**

That, for me, was worth everything.

2.4 Exploring Interests Before Chasing Marks

Most parents begin with the question, "What marks did you get?" Rarely do they ask, "What did you learn?" or "What excited you this week?"

Marks matter, yes. They open doors. But they **don't guarantee fulfillment or excellence**. A child who loves what they do will ultimately outperform others—even if their academic start is slow.

Parents must:

- Allow space for interests to evolve.
- Help children try different things early.
- Give exposure to real-life careers—not just classroom subjects.
- Invest in trial and error, without judgment.

2.5 Realistic vs. Aspirational Goals: Striking the Right Balance

It's natural for parents to want the best. But we must ask—**is our goal realistic, aspirational, or delusional?**

Aspirational Goals are:

- Slightly above current performance.
- Stretching, but attainable with effort.
- Aligned with the child's interests and strengths.

Realistic Goals are:

- Grounded in current capability and behavior.
- Built with an understanding of learning pace and temperament.

Delusional Goals are:

- Based on comparisons (e.g., "Sharma's son is a doctor.")
- Far beyond the child's current academic or emotional ability.
- Imposed without checking interest or readiness.

For example:

- Expecting a child who struggles with science to crack NEET without passion or aptitude is setting them up for years of pressure.
- Forcing a commerce-loving child into engineering because it sounds secure is planting seeds of resentment.

Instead, parents should look at:

- **Academic performance patterns**
- **Learning styles**
- **Extra-curricular interests**
- **Social and emotional maturity**

Aspirations must be pursued **with strategy, not blind pressure.**

2.6 Peer Pressure and Parental Influence: The Double-Edged Sword

Peer pressure plays a massive role in student choices:

- "Everyone is doing IIT coaching. I'll join too."
- "My friends are taking Bio. Maybe I should, too."

But beneath that, lies an even **bigger influence—parental pressure.**

Sometimes, **parents project their own unfulfilled dreams** onto their children:

- "I wanted to become a doctor, but couldn't. Now you must."
- "Engineering is safe and secure—go for it."

Other times, parents succumb to **society's scoreboard**:

- "What will people say if my child takes arts?"
- "All our relatives' kids are in IITs—we can't be the odd ones out."

This leads to a **toxic loop**: Children make career decisions to **please others**, not because they are passionate about them.

The result?

- Dropouts
- Burnouts
- Job dissatisfaction
- Constant self-doubt

Parents must break this cycle. The goal is not to chase popularity—but to **nurture purpose**.

2.7 A Heartbreaking Case: The Archery Champion That Could Have Been

One of the most heartbreaking stories I've personally witnessed was that of a friend's son—a naturally gifted **archer**.

This child had won medals in school-level competitions, was passionate, and had a coach who believed in him. But his father had a job that demanded transfers every few years. Archery was seen as "just a hobby."

Without stability or coaching, the child dropped out of training. His talent faded. His dream died.

I often wonder—*what if his parents had created a support structure?*

What if they had found a way to prioritize this one gift?

Would we have had another Olympic gold for India?

This is why **parental sacrifice matters.** If a child's true talent is identified—**nothing else matters more**. Time, money, effort—**everything must be channeled** to help them rise.

2.8 Final Thoughts: The Parent's Promise

Dear parents, your child doesn't need you to plan their entire future.

They need you to:

- Watch them closely.
- Listen without judgment.
- Encourage them to explore.
- Be patient when they fail.
- Believe in their uniqueness.
- Guide without controlling.

Be the one person in their life who allows them to grow into who they really are.

Because a child who is supported in their core talent will not only succeed—they will **shine, inspire, and lead.**

Chapter Summary: Key Messages

Guiding Principle	Parent's Role
Enable, don't enforce	Create a discovery ecosystem
Expose early	Let children try and fail safely
Watch, don't push	Observe interest patterns
Prioritize interest over prestige	Don't chase peer approval
Balance realism and aspiration	Avoid delusional targets
Commit deeply if talent is found	Go all in—time, money, and energy
Protect dreams from peer and social pressure	Be their shield and cheerleader

Chapter 3

Understanding Strengths, Not Just Subjects

"A mark sheet may reveal a grade, but it can never reveal a gift."

3.1 Introduction: The Hidden Gap in Today's Education

When a child scores 95 in Math or 90 in Science, the world often applauds without hesitation. These numbers become badges of honor, conversation starters at family gatherings, and even yardsticks of parenting success. However, when the same child paints a beautiful portrait, composes a soulful melody, or designs a game level using free software, it's rarely celebrated with the same enthusiasm. Most times, it is viewed as a hobby—something secondary, optional, or even a distraction.

Our education system—and unfortunately, even our home environments—often reduce a child's identity to a set of academic subjects. The evaluation is limited to Math, Science, English, and Social Science. But who the child is, what makes them shine, what they are naturally inclined toward—these deeper truths often get lost in the shadows.

This chapter aims to shift the lens. We need to move beyond viewing students through their subject scores and begin seeing them through the lens of their unique strengths and individual traits. Every child is born with a natural inclination towards certain skills and sensibilities. Identifying and nurturing these strengths early can set the foundation for a life filled with purpose and fulfillment.

3.2 What Are Strengths? (Hint: Not Just Subject Scores)

A strength is not merely something a child performs well in academics. It is a deeper, more nuanced trait that blends natural ability, interest, and emotional connection. A strength is where a child's skills and their joy intersect. It is something they do well, enjoy doing, and find easy to improve in over time. True strengths are marked by a sense of flow—the child becomes engrossed, loses track of time, and gains energy from the activity instead of feeling drained.

Some examples of such strengths include logical reasoning, creativity, empathy, or spatial intelligence. These may manifest outside the boundaries of traditional school subjects. For instance, a child with excellent observation skills may become a great wildlife photographer or detective, while one who loves organizing events may grow into a stellar project manager or entrepreneur. Recognizing strengths as something beyond academic scores helps lay the path to meaningful careers and lives.

3.3 The Mistake of Subject-Centric Evaluation

Unfortunately, many students who don't score well in school subjects are automatically labeled as average or underperformers. This labeling can deeply impact a child's self-worth and future decisions. But what if the measurement itself is flawed? What if we are measuring memory instead of intelligence, exam performance instead of curiosity, and conformity instead of creativity?

A child who scores 60 in Science but creates a working robot from watching online videos is anything but weak. A girl who struggles with math but choreographs original and moving dance routines is far from average. A boy who is quiet in class yet writes stunning short stories in his notebook has a deep inner world waiting to be nurtured. These examples show us how the traditional evaluation systems fail to capture the full spectrum of a child's potential. Our goal should not be to squeeze every child into a mold, but to understand and support their uniqueness.

3.4 From My Son to the Drums: A Lesson in Pattern Recognition

Let me take you through a personal journey that illustrates the essence of this chapter. With my son, Sudharshan, I embarked on an exploration to understand where his real interests and strengths lay. I tried exposing him to various sports—football, skating, and tennis—but he didn't resonate with any of them. I tried music too; first the guitar, which didn't hold his attention. Then the keyboard, which he found too mechanical. Just when I was wondering what else to try, I noticed something subtle—his constant tapping of fingers on tables, his rhythm when he walked, and how he naturally responded to music beats.

It was then that I enrolled him in drum lessons. The change was immediate and profound. He felt at home. His posture changed. His attention span increased. He was alive in those classes. That was the moment I realized that strength often reveals itself in patterns—subtle, repetitive behaviors that show up over time. This journey with my son taught me that strengths are not always obvious; they often need careful, patient observation.

3.5 Strengths May Be Subtle, But They Speak

One of the biggest challenges in recognizing strengths is that they rarely announce themselves loudly. Some children may be shy, introverted, or less expressive, and their strengths often whisper rather than shout. But those whispers are always there—hidden in how they spend their free time, in the kind of books or videos they're drawn to, in the way they explain things to others, or in what excites them the most.

For example, a child who quietly watches YouTube videos on interior decoration may have a visual-spatial strength. One who builds intricate LEGO sets may have strong engineering instincts. Another who helps mediate fights among siblings or classmates could grow into a capable negotiator or counselor. Our role as parents and educators is to pay attention to these signs and avoid dismissing them as childish whims. Every subtle cue is a clue toward discovering a child's true potential.

3.6 Strengths vs. Passion vs. Interest: What's the Difference?

It's important to distinguish between three concepts that are often used interchangeably: interest, passion, and strength. An **interest** is usually the starting point—it is what a child is curious about or enjoys casually. A child may show interest in painting for a few weeks and then move on to something else. A **passion** is a deeper, more consistent engagement. It is something a child is emotionally invested in and keeps returning to. A **strength**, on the other hand, is what a child is naturally good at, often without much effort.

Sometimes all three align, and that's ideal. But often they don't. A child may be passionate about cricket but lack the physical endurance to play professionally. Or a child may be very strong in math but not feel any excitement doing it. The key is to explore all three and help the child make informed choices. When strength and passion align, and interest is sustained, the child is far more likely to find long-term success and happiness.

3.7 Why Strengths Matter More in the Long Run

In the long run, once children step out into college or the real world, marks begin to fade into the background. What truly matters is their ability to think independently, adapt to challenges, collaborate with others, and innovate when needed. All these abilities stem from their innate strengths. A child who knows their strengths grows up with greater confidence and clarity. They are less likely to chase careers based on external validation and more likely to pursue paths that bring internal fulfillment.

Furthermore, identifying and working on strengths early prevents burnout. Children are not forced into directions that drain them. They find joy in their pursuits and meaning in their progress. Strength-based education and parenting lead to self-aware individuals who are equipped not just to survive but to thrive in an ever-changing world.

3.8 How to Help Your Child Discover Their Strengths

Here are five practical ways that parents can actively support the process of discovering and nurturing their child's strengths:

1. **Observation, Not Judgment:** Start by being an observer. Watch how your child behaves in various settings—when they are relaxed, when they are with friends, or when they are problem-solving. What kind of games do they enjoy? What topics do they talk about passionately? This quiet observation is often more powerful than any test or report card.

2. **Diverse Exposure:** Expose children to as many different experiences as possible—coding camps, painting workshops, robotics clubs, public speaking courses, sports, cooking, music classes. Every new activity is an opportunity for self-discovery. The more varied the exposure, the more refined the understanding of the child's inclinations.

3. **Conversations Over Commands:** Instead of constantly instructing children on what to do, try engaging them in meaningful conversations. Ask open-ended questions like, "What did you enjoy most this week?", "If you could spend a whole day doing anything, what would it be?", or "What problem in the world would you like to solve?" These questions can reveal hidden passions and strengths.

4. **Seek External Feedback:** Sometimes teachers, relatives, or even peers notice talents that parents may miss. Be open to feedback from others, especially when multiple people notice the same strengths in your child. This external validation can often reinforce your own observations.

5. **Professional Assessments:** If you're unsure, consider professional psychometric assessments. These tools are designed to evaluate learning styles, personality traits, and career orientation. While they shouldn't be the sole factor in decision-making, they can serve as useful guides when interpreted by professionals.

3.9 Strengths May Change – That's Okay!

It is important to understand that strengths can evolve. A child may show a flair for music at the age of 10 and later develop an interest in technology or leadership by the age of 15. This evolution is natural and should be encouraged. Strengths are not permanent labels but starting points for exploration.

What matters most is that children are encouraged to pursue what feels meaningful and energizing at each stage of their development. By allowing flexibility, we teach children that growth is a journey and not a fixed destination. We also allow them to reinvent themselves with confidence instead of guilt.

3.10 Final Message: See the Child, Not Just the Student

Dear parents, your child is not just a student enrolled in a school. They are a whole human being with a unique inner world, full of strengths, dreams, fears, and curiosities. Their true potential will not be revealed by a report card or rank list. It will be revealed through your love, attention, and willingness to see them for who they truly are.

Your role is to help them explore fearlessly, celebrate small wins, support them in failures, and guide them towards a life where they are in harmony with their strengths. A child aligned with their core strengths is not just more likely to succeed—they are more likely to be happy, confident, and emotionally resilient.

Chapter Summary: Key Takeaways

Concept	Message
Strength ≠ Subject	Strength is a natural ability, not a school subject
Observe Patterns	Look at what your child does consistently and happily
Don't Rush Labels	Strengths evolve—support growth, not judgment
Build Confidence	Strength awareness leads to self-esteem and clarity
Let Them Shine	Every child has a light—don't dim it with comparison

CHAPTER 4

The Myth of the 'Only One Path'

*"There is no single formula for success—and it's time we stopped
pretending there is."*

4.1 The Glut in Engineering and Medical Streams

India has long held engineering and medicine as the gold standard for
career success. Yet the past two decades have witnessed an unchecked
explosion in the number of engineering and medical colleges across
the country. Fueled by the aspirations of middle-class families and the
social prestige associated with these professions, this rapid expansion
has had unintended consequences.

Take engineering as a case in point:

- Over **3,500 engineering colleges** operate in India.
- Every year, **1.5 million engineers** graduate, but only **15-20%**
  are truly employable in their field.
- The market, however, doesn't generate a proportionate number
  of engineering jobs.

This leads to a grim reality: thousands of engineering graduates,
after spending **four crucial years** of their life and ₹6 to ₹10 **lakhs**
on education and living expenses, end up taking jobs unrelated to
their degrees. It is now common to see engineers working as **delivery
partners for Swiggy or Zomato,** as **sales executives in banks,** or in
low-paying BPO jobs—all roles that do not require a technical degree.

This is not to demean these jobs but to highlight the **tragic mismatch**
between investment and outcome. When a family spends years preparing

a child for engineering—through coaching, tuitions, and emotional support—only to see them land a job that pays ₹15,000 to ₹25,000 per month, the return on investment is not just poor—it's devastating.

4.2 The Illusion of Stability and Prestige

Parents often view these degrees as passports to financial security. But the reality is starkly different:

- **Curricula are outdated**, disconnected from real-world industry needs.
- **Infrastructure and faculty** quality in many private colleges are subpar.
- **Campus placements** are poor or nonexistent, especially outside of Tier 1 institutions.

Only the top 5-10%—those graduating from IITs, NITs, or highly reputed private institutions—are able to secure jobs in their domain. The rest are left to fend for themselves, often shifting to unrelated fields or spending years preparing for government exams or trying to re-skill through online platforms.

We are effectively **mass-producing engineers without a plan**, leaving them in a saturated job market with dwindling prospects.

4.3 The Hidden Costs: Emotional and Psychological

Aside from the financial burden, these misguided choices often result in emotional burnout and mental health issues:

- Students who were never inclined towards engineering or medicine find themselves trapped in joyless academic programs.
- The failure to get a job in the chosen field often leads to a **loss of self-esteem** and **feelings of inadequacy**.

- Parents too feel the pressure and disappointment when their massive investments don't yield expected returns.

The phrase "At least get the degree" has become a form of emotional insurance for parents, but it comes at the cost of a child's potential and passion.

4.4 Exploring Alternate High-Potential Careers

The world has evolved, and with it, so have career opportunities. It's time to shed the outdated belief that only doctors and engineers lead stable, respected lives. Here are some alternate career paths that are not only viable but are in **high demand**:

- **Digital Marketing** – With every brand going online, digital marketing is a booming industry.
- **UX/UI Design** – The design of user interfaces can make or break a product.
- **Animation and Game Design** – With the explosion of gaming and entertainment, this field is flourishing.
- **Data Science and Business Analytics** – Skill-based and lucrative, this is one of the most in-demand fields.
- **Mental Health Professionals** – The rising awareness of mental wellness has opened new avenues for psychology graduates.
- **Social Media Management and Influencing** – Building a personal brand has become a career of its own.
- **Trades and Vocational Skills** – Electricians, plumbers, automotive technicians, and similar vocations continue to see steady demand and offer good pay.
- **Entrepreneurship** – With start-up ecosystems flourishing, many youths are now creating their own paths instead of following traditional ones.

4.5 Success Stories from Unconventional Backgrounds

Let's take inspiration from those who chose the road less traveled:

- **Bhuvan Bam** – With no formal training in media, he started with a smartphone camera and a sense of humor. Today, he is a multi-millionaire content creator and entrepreneur.
- **Ranveer Allahbadia (BeerBiceps)** – Trained as an engineer, he switched to fitness coaching, and later, podcasting. Today, he runs one of India's top content channels and a successful media company.
- **Kiran Mazumdar-Shaw** – Initially a brewer, she transformed Biocon into one of India's leading biopharmaceutical companies despite societal resistance.
- **Vani Kola** – After a successful tech career in Silicon Valley, she returned to India to become a leading venture capitalist, funding India's next generation of entrepreneurs.

These stories underline that success doesn't follow a fixed formula. It favors those who understand their strengths, adapt to change, and are willing to step off the beaten path.

4.6 The Takeaway for Parents and Students

- **Think beyond tradition**: Engineering and medicine are not the only respectable professions.
- **Evaluate ROI**: Understand the financial and time investment versus likely outcomes.
- **Focus on skills, not just degrees**: Many modern careers value **what you can do** over **what you studied**.
- **Give children space to explore**: Encourage hobbies, internships, and creative projects early on.

In a world that's changing faster than ever before, sticking to only one path is not just limiting—it's risky. We need to prepare our children for **opportunity-rich** futures, not past ideas of success.

CHAPTER 5

Identifying Natural Strengths Early

"Don't ask what the world needs. Ask what makes you come alive—and go do it."

5.1 Simple Tools for Aptitude Identification

Identifying natural strengths should ideally begin in the formative school years, between Classes 6 and 12. This is when students begin to exhibit unique traits, skills, and preferences. Some may naturally lean toward storytelling, others toward numbers, and still others toward building, organizing, or artistic expression. Unfortunately, many of these tendencies go unnoticed due to a lack of structured observation, standardized assessments, or an enabling environment that encourages curiosity and self-exploration.

Today, there are a variety of tools that can help uncover a student's innate abilities. Psychometric assessments, interest inventories, and multiple intelligence tests such as DMIT (Dermatoglyphics Multiple Intelligence Test) offer broad indicators of aptitude and cognitive style. These tools evaluate logical reasoning, linguistic ability, spatial intelligence, interpersonal skills, and more. Though no test is foolproof or absolute, they provide valuable clues for parents and teachers. Investing in a certified career counselor who can administer and interpret these tests meaningfully can change the trajectory of a student's journey.

In addition to formal tools, a powerful method for aptitude discovery lies in day-to-day observation. A child who enjoys categorizing their books, making checklists, or planning events may have managerial or analytical skills. Another child who is naturally empathetic and enjoys helping others might thrive in counseling, teaching, or medicine. Parents and educators need to record, reflect, and refine their understanding of these behavioral patterns over time. A structured journal or periodic review sessions can help trace a student's evolving interests.

5.2 Learning Styles and How They Affect Career Paths

Not all students learn the same way. One of the most overlooked aspects in education and career planning is the diversity of learning styles. These are the unique methods by which individuals absorb, process, and retain information. Understanding a child's learning style can illuminate the best academic paths and future professions for them.

- **Visual learners** absorb information best when it is presented in pictures, diagrams, or mind maps. These students often excel in fields like architecture, graphic design, fashion, or engineering where visual thinking is paramount.
- **Auditory learners** prefer listening to lectures, podcasts, and discussions. Careers in law, radio, teaching, music, and counseling may come naturally to them.
- **Kinesthetic learners** learn through physical movement and hands-on experiences. They often thrive in areas such as sports, event management, medical procedures, and craftsmanship.

When parents and schools tailor learning strategies to suit these styles, students experience greater engagement, better retention, and more enthusiasm for studies. More importantly, when students understand how they learn best, they gain confidence and are more likely to pursue careers aligned with their natural mode of thinking.

5.3 Role of Mentors and School Counselors

The value of mentorship cannot be overstated in the early stages of career exploration. Mentors and counselors serve as guiding lights, helping students understand themselves and the opportunities available to them. Unfortunately, most Indian schools treat career counseling as a one-off event in Class 10 or 12 rather than an ongoing developmental process.

A good mentor listens, questions, challenges, and encourages. Whether it's a teacher, a senior student, a professional in the family, or an external coach, mentors help broaden a student's horizons beyond marks and mainstream choices. They introduce students to real-world applications of their interests and abilities.

School counselors, if present and well-trained, can assess emotional and academic needs, administer interest and aptitude tests, and provide age-appropriate guidance. Their role becomes crucial in:

- Introducing students to diverse career options they may not be aware of
- Offering clarity on subject selection and extracurricular engagement
- Building soft skills like communication, decision-making, and time management

Moreover, schools should integrate career exploration into the regular curriculum from middle school onward. Interaction with professionals, field visits, and project-based learning guided by mentors can help students visualize their future pathways more vividly.

5.4 Why Early Identification Matters

Most students in India are asked the big question—"What do you want to become?"—only during Class 10 or 12, often under pressure and without adequate preparation. This late inquiry leads to hasty decisions, stress, and misaligned career choices. By identifying interests and aptitudes early, students can explore, refine, and develop relevant skills without pressure.

Early identification offers a range of benefits:

- **Skill Development Over Time:** A child interested in writing can be encouraged to contribute to school magazines, participate in storytelling contests, or start a blog. Over time, this leads to both competence and confidence.
- **Motivation Through Alignment:** When children pursue what they love and are good at, their internal motivation grows. They no longer need external pressure to study or practice.
- **Academic Clarity:** Knowing their interests allows students to choose academic subjects and extracurricular activities with a sense of purpose.
- **Mental Well-being:** When expectations match abilities, stress reduces, self-worth increases, and academic anxiety diminishes.

We must stop treating career planning as an emergency response in adolescence and instead view it as a natural evolution of a child's identity from the early years.

5.5 The Parent's Role in Discovery

The journey of identifying a child's potential is a marathon, not a sprint. As a parent, I've experienced firsthand the patience and trial-and-error involved in this process. Once again I would emphasise my experience with my son, Sudharshan, I explored multiple avenues—sports like football, skating, and tennis—before realizing he didn't connect deeply with any of them. I then introduced musical instruments: guitar came and went, but it was the drums that finally lit a spark in him.

This journey taught me two powerful lessons. First, you cannot force a child to excel in something that doesn't resonate with their inner calling. Games, art, and music are not skills to be implanted— they emerge from within, possibly carried over from a previous life or shaped by deep-seated temperament. Second, discovery is only possible through exposure. Had I not experimented with different activities, I might never have discovered his love for rhythm.

Parents must become facilitators and observers rather than enforcers. Offer a buffet of experiences, and allow the child to express preferences. Watch how they respond, what sustains their interest, and what they talk about with excitement. Avoid pushing them into careers for the sake of prestige, social comparison, or parental ego.

I also want to emphasize the sacrifices involved. If your child's strength lies in music, sports, or another niche area, you must be willing to invest time, money, and emotional energy to help them pursue excellence. I've seen a friend's son who was brilliant at archery miss out on a potential Olympic career because frequent transfers disrupted his training. The opportunity was lost not due to lack of talent, but due to circumstantial neglect. Such stories are painful reminders of what's at stake when talent isn't nurtured properly.

5.6 Final Thoughts

Identifying natural strengths is not about preparing children for exams, but for life. It's about understanding who they are, not who we want them to be. It's about preparing them for a future where passion and competence intersect to create joy, success, and meaning.

Instead of asking, "What will make my child successful?", let us begin to ask, "What makes my child come alive?" The answer to that question is the compass that will guide them to their purpose.

> *"When talent meets opportunity, magic happens. Let's be the enablers of that magic."*

Conclusion – Foundations: The Early Crossroads

The early crossroads in life often come silently—without a warning sign or a defined moment of clarity. And yet, these moments hold the power to shape everything that follows. In this foundational phase, where students stand at the delicate threshold between curiosity and commitment, the choices they make—or are guided to make—can either unlock their true potential or unintentionally stifle it.

This section has journeyed through the crucial layers that influence early career decision-making—starting with the raw confusion of young minds trying to navigate choices, the often well-meaning but sometimes overbearing influence of parents, the importance of identifying true strengths over textbook knowledge, the dangers of chasing a single "perfect path," and the unmatched power of recognizing natural abilities early in life.

At this stage, the emphasis must shift from simply "what to become" to "who you are becoming." Students must be encouraged to explore their inclinations, passions, and innate talents without the burden of fitting into preset molds. Equally, parents and educators must evolve from being decision-makers to **enablers of self-discovery**. The narrative must change from dictating a future to co-creating a vision with empathy and patience.

We must remember that no two journeys are the same. Success does not arrive by choosing a traditionally respected path, but by walking a path that resonates with one's own calling—even if it's unconventional. A student with a deep love for drawing may bring more value to the world through design or animation than by being forced into a degree they cannot relate to. A young adult who enjoys fixing things might have the makings of a great engineer, mechanic, or innovator—regardless of the marks in math. Early recognition of such passions, with the right nurturing, can lead to extraordinary outcomes.

Just as foundations determine the strength of any structure, the thoughts, encouragements, questions, and experiments of these early years form the blueprint for the future. These are the years where confidence is either built or broken. Where comparisons can kill curiosity, and where freedom can fuel excellence.

As we close this part of the journey, let's remember: every young mind deserves a chance to discover—not just a career, but themselves. Let's not rush them to decide who they want to be for the rest of their lives before they've even figured out who they are today. Let us instead inspire them to observe, reflect, and explore with openness, because the **right direction is often born not from pressure, but from awareness**.

Foundations, when built right, don't just support careers—they shape lives.

PART II

THE CAMPUS YEARS: EXPLORATION & REALIGNMENT

Audience: College Students, Young Adults

The college years are often painted as a time of freedom, fun, and friendships—but they're also one of the most pivotal phases in shaping a person's life trajectory. These years are far more than a bridge between school and employment—they are a crucible of transformation, self-discovery, and foundational growth. For many students, college is the first time they step out of their familiar cocoon. It's when they begin to question, explore, and encounter the world beyond the black-and-white of textbooks and examinations.

This is the phase where young adults must learn to balance expectations with ambition, practicality with passion. The classroom certainly offers lessons—but the bigger classroom is life itself, unfolding all around. During these years, real learning happens when students step outside their comfort zones: when they take up internships, volunteer in unfamiliar environments, travel to unknown places, join student-led initiatives, or even attempt side projects that might never be graded but will surely be remembered.

Unfortunately, many students fall into the trap of routine—attending classes, writing exams, chasing marks—without realizing that the world beyond college requires more than academic knowledge. It requires adaptability, confidence, communication skills, and above all, self-awareness. That awareness doesn't come from memorizing answers. It comes from experiences, from failures, from rejections, and from finding one's way through detours and doubts.

This section is about **exploration with intent**—not just randomly trying things, but engaging in purposeful experiences that can help shape identity, refine interests, and build capabilities. It's about **realignment**—because sometimes, the career we think we want in our first year of college is not the one we eventually pursue. And that's okay. In fact, that's normal. Life has a way of gently (or sometimes abruptly) nudging us toward paths we never imagined, but that turn out to be more fulfilling than our original plan.

Here, we will dive into real stories and practical reflections—how internships and part-time jobs can open new doors; how travel exposes students to diversity and perspective; how failing a campus placement or being rejected for a dream job might be the very thing that redirects a student to their true calling. We will also talk about the importance of resisting the "herd mentality" and learning to listen to one's inner compass amidst all the noise and pressure of campus life.

More than anything, this part encourages students and young adults to **own their journey**. To be bold enough to try, to fail, and to pivot. To be humble enough to accept that they don't have all the answers yet— and wise enough to know that that's perfectly fine. Because the campus years are not just about building a resume—they are about **building the person behind that resume**.

So, let us explore, reflect, and realign—with open eyes, open minds, and an open heart.

CHAPTER 6

The Power of Exposure

There are phases in life where the direction you take can redefine everything about your future. For students and young adults, the college years represent such a phase—not because of exams or degrees, but because of the **immense opportunity for exposure** they provide. These years are not just about attending lectures, writing papers, or scoring high marks. They are about **discovering the world and discovering yourself**.

Many students make the mistake of treating college as a continuation of school: a routine path of attendance, note-taking, and exam preparation. But those who look beyond that shell—who dare to step out into the real world—find something extraordinary. They find life lessons that can't be taught in classrooms. They find passions that were hidden beneath expectations. They find confidence that comes only from experience. And most importantly, they find **purpose**.

In this chapter, we explore why **exposure** is a more valuable asset than grades. And how internships, volunteering, travel, and side projects can provide clarity, character, and confidence—far beyond what marks ever could.

Time is Gold, Not Just Money

There's a popular saying: "Time is money." But for young people in college, time is **gold**—far more valuable than currency. Money can be earned, spent, lost, and regained. But time, once gone, never returns. This is the most energetic, open-minded, and fearless phase of life. Yet many students either waste it in over-reliance on their academic curriculum or stay too focused on immediate comfort zones.

One of the most critical realizations that young adults must have is this: **merely attending college will not give you real-world experience**. Sitting in lectures might give you theoretical knowledge, but it does not equip you to handle the dynamism, ambiguity, and unpredictability of the world outside.

This is the time to experiment, to learn by doing, and to fail gracefully. Whether you come from an affluent background or a modest one, this phase is not about making money—it's about building yourself. You may never get another chance in life where you can explore without consequences. So take the leap. Stretch your boundaries.

Internships: Learning from the Ground Up

One of the best ways to gain real exposure is through **internships**. Whether during summer breaks or as part of a semester program, internships are your ticket into the real world. Even a few weeks of shadowing professionals, handling actual tasks, and understanding workplace culture can open your eyes to what lies ahead.

Internships are not just about adding a line to your resume. They help you:

- Understand industry expectations.
- Build soft skills like communication, discipline, and teamwork.
- Learn how to handle responsibilities and deadlines.
- Discover what roles and industries excite you—and which ones don't.

You may find that the career you thought was your dream isn't the right fit after experiencing it firsthand. That realization itself is a powerful insight, saving you years of confusion later. Whether you intern at a startup, a corporate company, or even a social enterprise— every experience adds to your growth.

And remember, **you don't have to be paid to gain value**. Internships offer something more precious: **wisdom through exposure**.

Volunteering: Cultivating Compassion and Responsibility

Volunteering is another underrated but powerful avenue. When you step into social causes or community initiatives—be it through NGOs, college-led campaigns, or independent projects—you learn to operate from a place of empathy. You understand society's deeper layers: inequality, education gaps, healthcare needs, environmental concerns, and more.

Volunteering helps you:

- Develop a broader worldview.
- Improve your leadership and people-management skills.
- Feel the satisfaction of contributing beyond yourself.
- Connect with passionate individuals from diverse walks of life.

The impact of volunteering is lifelong. You may spend just a few hours a week, but the values and perspectives you gain remain with you forever.

Travel: The University of the World

If the classroom is where you learn theories, then **travel is where you experience life**. Every place has a culture. Every journey offers a lesson. Travelling during college—whether alone or with friends—pushes you into unfamiliar situations. You learn to navigate new environments, interact with strangers, budget your money, plan logistics, and deal with uncertainties.

But more importantly, **you learn about people**. Their habits, beliefs, fears, and hopes. You develop patience, adaptability, and humility. You begin to see the world not just through your lens, but through the lens of others. And that changes you deeply.

Travel can be:

- A weekend trip to a historical town.
- A volunteering stint in a rural village.

- A cultural exchange program abroad.
- A solo backpacking adventure with just a notebook and a backpack.

Each journey is a story, a memory, a lesson—and sometimes, a turning point.

Side Projects: Where Passion Meets Action

While college projects may be part of your syllabus, **side projects are born from curiosity**. They reflect what truly excites you. Maybe it's building a mobile app. Writing a blog. Designing posters. Starting a YouTube channel. Creating music. Launching a college event. Or automating something in your neighborhood.

These projects show that **you can start something, own it, and complete it**. They teach initiative, ownership, teamwork, and the grit to overcome challenges. Employers, mentors, and future partners look at side projects as proof of passion. And you yourself will look back at them as defining moments of learning and pride.

A Real-Life Journey: Selling SIM Cards, Building Software, and Living Independently

Let me share a piece of my own journey—one that illustrates the power of using your time wisely during your campus years.

I was studying **B.Com in an evening college**. While many of my peers focused solely on academics, I had a dream: I wanted a **bike**. It was not just a vehicle; it was a symbol of independence and aspiration. There was no pressure on me to earn—my family supported me. But I felt a deep desire to do something on my own.

So, I joined **AirCel as a sales executive**, selling SIM cards. My day started at 7:00 AM. I'd be out on the streets, talking to shopkeepers, convincing customers, facing rejection, and learning how to sell. By

2:00 PM, I'd finish work, rush to my **computer classes from 3:00 PM to 5:00 PM**, and then attend college **from 5:30 PM to 8:00 PM**.

It was a packed schedule. Tiring, yes—but incredibly fulfilling.

In my second year, we had to complete a project for our computer course. I proposed to my team that instead of doing a standard theoretical assignment, we do a **real-time project**. We approached a reputed **catering college** in our town, observed their operations, and developed a custom software solution to automate their internal processes.

Within four months, the system was built and implemented. We submitted it for our project evaluation, where it received great feedback. But what happened next stunned us: the **Dean of the catering college invited me**, appreciated our work, and offered us **₹40,000 as a token of gratitude**.

That was 1998. ₹40,000 was a significant amount. But more than the money, what I received that day was **recognition, confidence, and belief** in my ability to contribute to the real world.

That experience taught me how to:

- **Manage time** across multiple priorities.
- **Balance work and study** without losing focus.
- **Take initiative** and lead a team.
- **Deliver results** in a real business environment.
- And most importantly, **trust myself**.

That moment was a turning point—and it happened not because of a classroom or a textbook, but because of **exposure**.

Conclusion: Become the Explorer of Your Own Life

Your college years are your lab. Your mind is curious. Your energy is boundless. This is not the time to hide behind marks or stay trapped in the safe zone. **This is the time to explore.**

Explore work. Explore people. Explore causes. Explore the world. Explore yourself.

Whether through internships, volunteering, travel, or side projects, you will begin to understand what excites you, what challenges you, and what gives your life meaning. That clarity will not come from textbooks. It will come from the field.

So go ahead—take that internship. Say yes to a volunteering campaign. Plan that travel. Build that idea. Take risks. Fail. Get up. Try again.

Because the greatest lessons of life are waiting for you outside the classroom. All you have to do is step out.

Ask Yourself these Questions and Answer to know you.

What are some side projects or interests you've been postponing? Can you start them now?

____

____

____

____

____

Have you ever taken up a part-time job or internship? If not, what's stopping you?

____

____

____

____

____

What kind of travel experiences do you think would help expand your perspective?

____

____

____

____

____

Can you list 3 causes or organizations where you'd love to volunteer?

____

____

____

____

____

What is one bold step you can take today to expose yourself to the real world?

____

____

____

____

____

Avoiding the "Herd Mentality" During Placements

"Just because everyone is running doesn't mean the direction
is right."

As college life approaches its final chapters, an atmosphere of urgency often takes over campuses. Placement season begins—not just a process but a **frenzy**. Students begin to move in a common direction, influenced more by peer pressure than purpose. Companies come and go, resumes are polished, suits are ironed, and career dreams begin to look identical. But this is where one of the greatest career pitfalls lies: the **herd mentality**.

What is Herd Mentality in Placements?

Herd mentality, in simple terms, is the tendency to follow what others are doing without questioning whether it suits your strengths, interests, or long-term goals. It manifests like this:

- Taking up a role just because your friends applied for it.
- Running behind a "big brand" without even understanding what the job entails.
- Accepting offers in fields you have no interest in, just to "not be left behind."
- Measuring your self-worth based on how many people got placed before you.

This mindset is dangerous—not because it leads to failure, but because it leads to **misalignment**. You may end up spending your prime years in jobs you don't like, working in industries that don't excite you, building skills that don't align with your aspirations.

Why the Herd Mentality Happens

There are several psychological and social triggers:

- **Fear of Missing Out (FOMO)** – You see your friends getting placed and fear you're falling behind.
- **Social Pressure** – Parents, peers, and faculty may all expect you to have a "placement story."
- **Insecurity** – You may not be sure of what you want, so you copy what others do.
- **Prestige Syndrome** – You feel it's more respectable to have a job—any job—than to explore alternatives or wait for the right one.

While all of these are understandable emotions, they can derail the most important decision of your early career: choosing the right **first step**.

How to Break Free from the Crowd

1. Know Your "Why"

Ask yourself:

- What am I naturally good at?
- What excites me—problem-solving, people interaction, design, numbers, leadership?
- What kind of environment do I thrive in—structured corporate setups or startup chaos?

Answering these helps you evaluate job opportunities based on *fit* rather than *FOMO*.

2. Research the Role, Not Just the Brand

Too many students chase company names without understanding job descriptions. A job at a top brand with no scope for growth or learning may hurt more than help. Evaluate:

- What are the day-to-day responsibilities?
- What will you learn in this role?
- Does it align with your long-term interests?

A lesser-known company with the right role is often more valuable than a famous one with the wrong fit.

3. Speak to Seniors and Alumni

Reach out to those who were once in your shoes. Ask them:

- What they wish they knew before placements.
- What their job turned out to be in reality.
- Whether they feel aligned with what they're doing.

Real stories bring real clarity.

4. Don't Be Afraid to Say No

It's okay to **wait** or **opt out** of a placement that doesn't suit your goals. Not having a job on Day 1 doesn't mean you're behind. It means you're thoughtful. If you have the financial or emotional space to take time, use it wisely to explore other options.

5. Explore Alternative Careers

Placements aren't the only route. Think about:

- Entrepreneurship
- Higher studies
- Government exams or specialized certifications
- Starting with internships in your dream field

This is your life, not a conveyor belt.

Real-Life Reflection: Choosing Your Own Path

Let me share a perspective here.

During my early career, I noticed several bright individuals enter fields that had nothing to do with their interests—just because they "got selected." Some were creative but went into data roles. Some were people-oriented but ended up in coding cubicles. Five years later, many of them were disillusioned or trying to switch careers entirely.

On the other hand, a few individuals **took the risk of listening to themselves**. One turned down a banking job and chose to work in an NGO for a year—eventually going on to build a successful career in international development. Another skipped placements altogether to build a startup, failed once, but is now a successful founder.

They trusted their **inner compass**. And that made all the difference.

The Long Game: Build a Life, Not Just a Career

Placement is a beginning, not a destination. What matters is not who gets placed first, but who finds alignment and joy in their work. A job taken in panic can cost you years. A job taken with clarity will shape your future.

"The best placement is not the one that comes fastest, but the one that fits best."

Closing Thoughts: Be Courageous. Be Curious. Be You.

In a world that rewards conformity, choosing your path is an act of courage. Don't let noise drown your voice. Reflect, research, and respond with intention—not impulse.

The crowd may be louder, but your inner voice is wiser. Listen to it.

Questions for your Reflection

1. Why do you want a job? Is it for experience, brand value, income, or learning?
2. What are 3 industries or roles you would genuinely enjoy working in?
3. What would you do if placements weren't mandatory?
4. Do you really understand what the job you're applying for *actually involves*?
5. Are you willing to wait or explore a better-aligned opportunity?

<h1>CHAPTER 7</h1>

The Role of Discipline – My NCC Experience

"Discipline is the bridge between goals and accomplishment."

– Jim Rohn

There are many moments in life that pass by unnoticed, and then there are those that define you—shape your thoughts, build your character, and mold your entire personality. For me, **my experience in the National Cadet Corps (NCC)** was one such defining chapter.

From my school days through to college, **NCC wasn't just an extracurricular activity—it was a way of life**. I didn't just wear the uniform; I lived the values it stood for. The khaki didn't just cover my body; it sank deep into my spirit and character. It taught me more than textbooks ever could—lessons that stayed with me long after the parades ended.

More Than Marching – The Discipline That Shapes You

When most people think of NCC, they imagine drills, parades, and camps. But for those of us who wore that badge proudly, it meant **discipline, commitment, responsibility, and self-respect**.

Waking up at 5:00 am, shining shoes until you could see your reflection, standing in attention under the blazing sun—it was never easy. But it wasn't about ease. It was about **training the mind and body to obey when it wants to give up**. It taught me **mental endurance**, something that would later help me in every walk of life—be it personal setbacks, tight project deadlines, or leadership dilemmas.

Even today, the lessons endure. I still don't step out of my house without polishing my shoes. That attention to detail, that sense of pride in appearance and order—it's deeply ingrained in me.

From Cadet to Leader – My Journey as Senior Under Officer

One of the most transformative roles I took on was that of an **Senior Under Officer**, first in school and later in college. It wasn't just a title; it was a responsibility to lead, inspire, and guide others. **Leadership, in NCC, is not about giving orders—it's about setting examples**.

As an Senior Under Officer, I learned:

- How to **manage a team under pressure**.
- How to ensure **unity in diversity**—working with cadets from different backgrounds and languages.
- How to lead a drill even when tired, how to motivate others when they felt like quitting.

These leadership qualities didn't stay behind on the parade ground. They became part of my professional identity. Today, as a business leader, I often draw from those same instincts—**lead by example, care for your team, and always stay prepared.**

A Medal Around My Neck, But More So In My Mind

One of my proudest moments was when I emerged as a **sharp shooter** in NCC. Winning medals gave me external validation, but more than the medal, it was the process of *becoming* a sharpshooter that mattered.

It taught me:

- **Focus under pressure.**
- The importance of **silence, stillness, and patience.**
- That hitting a bullseye is not about muscle, but about **mental control**.

In the rush of today's world, those lessons still help me—when I need to make critical decisions, when I need to center myself amidst chaos, when I need to find focus in noise.

Love for Nation – Not Just a Phrase, But a Feeling

Perhaps the deepest and most sacred lesson NCC gave me was the **love for my country**. Patriotism wasn't just about saluting the flag; it was about conducting oneself in a way that brought pride to the nation. Whether it was cleaning up our surroundings during Swachh Bharat initiatives or standing guard during Republic Day celebrations, **NCC made me feel responsible—not just for myself, but for the country.**

Even though I had an opportunity to move into the **National Defence Academy (NDA)** through NCC, personal constraints didn't allow me to pursue it. But I hold no regrets—because **the values and spirit of a soldier still live within me.** Every act of discipline, every job I do with integrity, every honest decision I take in my professional journey is, in some way, a tribute to the uniform I once wore.

Physical and Mental Toughness – A Lifelong Asset

NCC placed a strong emphasis on **fitness**—not just physical, but mental as well. From endurance drills to obstacle courses, from night treks to silent camps—these experiences tested us in ways we never imagined. And every time we made it through, **we were not the same person anymore—we were stronger, more resilient, more self-aware.**

This became my foundation. Even today, when I face tough times or complex challenges in my work, I don't panic. I assess, I plan, I act. And I carry within me a calmness that I learned under a scorching sun in a dusty training ground—where I first learned to **push beyond limits**.

Grooming, Dignity & Discipline in Daily Life

Many people underestimate the value of good grooming. But NCC taught me that **how you present yourself matters**. A clean uniform, polished shoes, an upright posture—these are not vanity, but symbols of discipline and respect.

Even now:

- I check my shoes before I leave home.
- I stand tall when I speak.
- I keep my space tidy and organized.

These may seem small, but they create a ripple effect. They build trust, they invite respect, and they instill **self-worth**.

Lessons That Travel With You for Life

To summarize, my NCC experience was not just a school or college phase—it was a **life education**. It taught me:

- **Discipline is not punishment; it's preparation.**
- **Leadership is not about commanding; it's about caring.**
- **Patriotism is not a date on the calendar; it's a daily choice.**
- **Mental and physical strength is your true armor in life.**
- **Respect begins with how you carry yourself.**

NCC didn't just make me a better student or a better professional. It made me a **better person**—more grounded, more grateful, and more giving.

"Once a cadet, always a cadet."

No matter where life takes me, the cadet in me still marches on—with discipline in my steps, love for my country in my heart, and a quiet pride that says: I lived the values of the uniform—and I still do.

CHAPTER 8

Learning from Rejection and Redirection

"Sometimes when things are falling apart, they may actually be falling into place."

In the grand journey of life and career, we are often taught to chase success, to celebrate wins, and to keep climbing upward. But what we aren't often taught is how to fall—and how to get back up with greater purpose and strength. This chapter is a tribute to those moments when things didn't go as planned, when the doors slammed shut, and when life whispered a gentle but firm "no."

Dealing with Failure, Detours, and Career Shifts

Failure is often perceived as a full stop—but in reality, it's just a comma in a long sentence. It's a pause, not the end. Everyone—yes, everyone—faces failure at some point. Whether it's being rejected in a campus interview, not making the cut for a dream university, or realizing that the job you thought you'd love isn't what you imagined—it's natural. What matters most is **how we respond to it.**

Early in life, our plans are neatly chalked out. "I'll do this course, get this job, and climb this ladder." But reality doesn't always honor our blueprint. Sometimes life throws detours—unexpected twists that force us to step off the highway and take the scenic route. While detours feel uncomfortable in the moment, they are often the best parts of the journey.

Career shifts, too, are often treated like taboo. "You studied commerce, why marketing now?" or "You worked in IT, why go into operations?" But the truth is—**evolution is natural**. Your interests change, your strengths emerge over time, and your purpose becomes clearer. A career shift isn't a sign of failure—it's a sign of awareness. It's a step toward **alignment**, not away from success.

Why Some "No"s Are Blessings in Disguise

We often see rejection as a personal blow, a statement on our worth. But the truth is, many of life's greatest opportunities come disguised as rejection.

That job interview you didn't crack? Maybe it saved you from a toxic workplace.

The course you didn't get into? Perhaps it nudged you toward a path you were truly meant for.

The promotion that didn't happen? It may have kept you available for a better role that needed you more.

Every "no" in life is a filter—eliminating the things that aren't meant for us, even if we don't understand it in the moment. In hindsight, we often thank those rejections. They gave us redirection.

Let's take a simple example. Think about all the famous people we admire—Amitabh Bachchan was once rejected by All India Radio for his voice. Steve Jobs was once removed from the very company he founded. J.K. Rowling was rejected by a dozen publishers before *Harry Potter* became a global sensation. What if they had stopped trying? What if they had believed that rejection meant "you're not good enough"?

The universe sometimes says "no" not because you don't deserve it, but because **you deserve something better**—something more aligned to your strengths, values, and purpose.

Rebuilding Confidence Post-Rejection

After rejection, it's natural to feel deflated. Confidence takes a hit. Self-doubt creeps in. You begin to question your worth, your talent, and your decisions. But this is the precise moment that defines your future—not the rejection itself, but your **response** to it.

Here's how you can begin to rebuild:

1. **Acknowledge the Pain** – Don't suppress it. It's okay to feel hurt or disappointed. Give yourself time to process.
2. **Separate Self-Worth from Outcome** – One rejection doesn't define who you are. Failure is an event, not an identity.
3. **Reflect, Don't Ruminate** – What can you learn from it? What could you do differently? What feedback did you receive?
4. **Recalibrate Your Compass** – Sometimes rejection is an indicator that it's time to pivot. Explore new paths with curiosity.
5. **Celebrate Small Wins** – Gain momentum by doing something you're good at. Build confidence by building action.

One of the most powerful things you can do after rejection is **keep moving**. Forward motion, even small steps, restores belief. And belief leads to resilience.

Personal Reflections: The Resilience Muscle

In my own life, I've faced rejections too—rejections that stung deeply. Opportunities I thought were tailor-made for me slipped through my fingers. Interviews where I had rehearsed everything perfectly still ended with a polite "we've moved forward with another candidate." But looking back, **each of those moments redirected me to something better**.

One detour led me to a job that opened doors I hadn't even dreamed of. One rejection gave me the courage to start my own initiative. Another helped me build patience—an underrated but powerful skill in a world obsessed with speed.

What I learned is that **rejection builds resilience**—and resilience is your true career capital. It's what separates those who give up from those who eventually break through.

Rejection is Redirection

To the young reader, the college student, or the early professional reading this—if you're dealing with rejection right now, know this: **you are not alone**. We've all been there. And many of us found our real calling not through perfect plans, but through imperfect, messy, heartbreaking detours.

Let every "no" push you to look deeper—into yourself and the world around you. Let it build you, not break you. Let it be a bend, not the end.

"Sometimes what didn't work out for you really worked out
for you."

You will grow from rejection. You will rise again. And someday, you'll look back and smile—not in pain, but with pride. Because what looked like the end was really the beginning.

CHAPTER 9

Choose Your Right Career Path

Stepping out of college is one of the most liberating yet confusing moments in a young adult's life. With a degree in hand, a thousand possibilities lie ahead—yet the clarity to choose the right one is often missing. It is at this critical juncture that many people either follow their heart or simply go with the flow. While both paths can lead to success, they are not equal in probability or purpose.

I speak from experience when I say that I chose to go with the flow. After college, I didn't have a clear-cut dream job. I entered the world of work with an open mind, learning and evolving through roles in Sales, Collections, Credit & Risk, and eventually Strategy. It was only after 16 years of solid ground-level experience that I arrived at what I truly love doing—leading technology-driven transformation in the banking sector. I enjoyed every step of the journey, but I recognize that not everyone gets the same chance. Some get lost in the routine, stuck in a role that doesn't resonate with who they are. Others simply never pause to reflect, and miss the chance to build a fulfilling career.

So how do you know which road to take?

Let me share a few real stories—people I've known closely—whose choices helped shape this perspective.

Gopinath – A Career by Design, Not by Default

Gopi, my brother's friend, studied BBA alongside him. From early on, his gift for public speaking and writing was evident. He had a natural flair for communication, and he nurtured it with passion. He dreamt of becoming a TV anchor—an uncommon path for someone from a conventional academic background. While others scrambled for bank jobs and corporate roles, Gopi struggled to find a footing in media. He took small gigs, faced many rejections, but never abandoned his passion.

One day, he got a break—a television debate show was looking for a fresh face. Gopi took the stage and left a lasting impression. His eloquence, sharp thinking, and deep knowledge earned him more opportunities. Today, he is a respected media personality, speaker, and host in Tamil Nadu—a true example of someone who **chose the road less traveled** and made it count. If he had taken the easier route—say, a bank job—he may have earned a stable income, but the world would've missed a unique voice, and he would have missed his calling.

Bala – A Childhood Dream Pursued with Purpose

Bala, my classmate, was academically brilliant and always spoke with clarity about his goal—he wanted to become a doctor. At 15, he had already charted his path. Unlike many who waver, he stuck to it with relentless focus. He cleared the medical entrance exams and today, he's one of the most renowned doctors in our city. His journey reaffirms that when your **career aligns with your passion and purpose early on**, success becomes a natural extension of your effort.

Arun – Going with the Flow

My friend Arun completed his MBA in Agriculture and joined a bank as a Management Trainee. He's smart, competent, and doing well in his role. But I often wonder: **what if** he had pursued a career in agribusiness or agricultural consulting—something he was academically and passionately equipped for? He might have thrived even more, possibly becoming a leader in the field. His decision to go with the flow got him stability, but perhaps at the cost of true professional satisfaction.

Pranav – Passion Lost in Translation

In my current organization, I work with Pranav, a transformation lead who holds an Aeronautical Mechanical Engineering degree. He is brilliant at what he does, but it's hard to ignore the mismatch between his education and his profession. If he had ventured into the aviation or engineering sector, his technical expertise might have led him to innovation or invention. While he excels in his current role, it raises a crucial question: **how often do people compromise their passion for instant gratification or convenience?**

Instant Gratification vs. Long-Term Fulfilment

One of the biggest reasons people choose the "go with the flow" route is **instant gratification**. The desire to earn immediately after college, to gain social validation, and to "settle down" often overrides deep introspection. Earning money becomes the only goal, and in that pursuit, people forget to ask the bigger question: *"Is this what I want to do for the next 30 years?"* This mindset might get you a job quickly, but it won't necessarily give you meaning, growth, or happiness in the long run.

A Movie That Speaks to This Truth

I'm reminded of the Tamil film **'Velaiyilla Pattathari'** where the protagonist Raghuvaran, a qualified civil engineer, is ridiculed and pressured at home for being unemployed. Despite many non-engineering job offers, he refuses to settle. The world sees him as idle and irresponsible, but he's waiting for the right opportunity—to work in the field he was trained for. Eventually, he lands the role of a civil engineer and goes on to build a successful career. The moral? **Patience, faith in oneself, and clarity of purpose can lead to extraordinary outcomes—even if the wait is painful.**

Guiding Principles: How to Choose the Right Career

1. **Know Your Inner Calling** Ask yourself: What am I naturally good at? What do I enjoy doing even when I'm not paid for it? Passion combined with skill is your true calling.
2. **Align Career with Core Strengths** Choose a path that allows your strengths to shine—be it creativity, analysis, empathy, communication, or problem-solving.
3. **Don't Chase Trends—Create Value** Just because everyone is doing coding or becoming a data analyst doesn't mean you should too. Trends change. True value remains.
4. **Avoid Short-Term Thinking** A job that pays well today but bores you to death tomorrow is not a win. Look at long-term satisfaction and growth potential.
5. **Explore Before You Commit** Internships, side projects, mentorships, and freelancing are tools to test different waters. Use them before making a full-time choice.
6. **Have the Courage to Say No** Sometimes, a tempting offer may not align with your goals. Don't be afraid to reject it if it takes you away from your path.
7. **Be Ready to Adapt, but Don't Settle** Careers evolve. You may not land your dream job on day one. But never lose sight of it. Keep realigning your steps toward your larger goal.
8. **Seek Mentors and Feedback** Don't decide alone. Speak to people in the fields you're interested in. Learn from their journeys and struggles.

What Do You Lose If You Don't?

- A sense of purpose in your work
- Fulfilment and joy that comes from doing what you love
- Time that cannot be regained once spent in the wrong path
- The chance to be exceptional, instead of just average

Final Thought

Choosing a career is not a race—it's a deeply personal decision that needs reflection, courage, and conviction. Go with the flow **only if** the flow aligns with who you are. Otherwise, take the harder path, the one that demands patience and perseverance. Because in the end, it's not just about getting a job. It's about building a life you won't regret.

Conclusion – The Campus Years: A Time to Shape, Shift, and Shine

As we close this section, one thing becomes crystal clear—the campus years are not merely a passage of time between adolescence and adulthood; they are the crucible in which one's personality, choices, and future are forged. These are not just years of academic pursuit, but a rich, transformative period filled with possibilities, missteps, and immense learning.

This is the time to test boundaries and step beyond the textbook. It is the phase to question the status quo, to explore the unfamiliar, and to give yourself the permission to try, fail, learn, and grow. Whether it is through internships, volunteering, working part-time, starting passion projects, or simply having meaningful conversations with diverse people, every experience counts. Every story, every rejection, every detour is silently molding you into someone wiser, stronger, and more self-aware.

You may not have all the answers today, and that is okay. In fact, these years are not about having it all figured out—they are about **figuring out what really matters to you**. They are about understanding your own inner voice amidst the crowd, learning how to take ownership of your choices, and gaining the courage to chart your own path—even if it looks different from what others expect.

The world will often try to box you into set definitions of success— placement packages, fancy degrees, societal approval. But the real victory lies in discovering what success means to *you* and pursuing it with sincerity and commitment. Let these years be the playground where you rehearse the life you want to live.

Remember, realignment is not failure—it is wisdom. The willingness to pause, reflect, and change direction is a sign of growth, not weakness. Be open to redirection. Embrace uncertainty. Learn from rejection. And above all, trust that every meaningful experience—whether exciting or painful—is contributing to the person you are becoming.

As you move toward the next phase of your life—whether it's stepping into the world of work, entrepreneurship, or further studies— carry the lessons of these years with pride. You are not just building a career; you are building **character, resilience, and purpose**.

Let your campus years be remembered not for how perfectly you followed a plan, but for how bravely you explored life beyond the plan.

A Pivotal Moment: Choosing the Right Career Path

The final chapter of this section—**"Choose Your Right Career Path"**— serves as the anchor that ties everything together. It is perhaps one of the most consequential decisions a young adult will make. After all the excitement of college fades and convocation ceremonies end, what lies ahead is a blank canvas. What you paint on it will define not just your career, but your happiness, mental well-being, sense of self-worth, and growth for decades to come.

In this chapter, we explored two dominant paths:

- **Going with the flow**—a path often chosen for immediate income, security, or societal pressure.
- **Choosing with intention**—a route aligned with one's passion, core strengths, and long-term goals.

We saw real stories of individuals who succeeded by staying true to their vision—like Gopinath, who turned his gift of speech into a successful media career, and Bali, who pursued his childhood dream of becoming a doctor with clarity and consistency. We also reflected on those who went with the flow, doing well but perhaps falling short of their full potential because of decisions made under the pressure of convenience or instant gratification.

We discussed how the wrong career choices—even if well-paying—can leave individuals disillusioned or stuck in roles that underutilize their true capabilities. On the other hand, choosing rightly, even if it demands struggle in the beginning, brings satisfaction, purpose, and eventually, success. As illustrated by the movie character Raghuvaran, patience and persistence in aligning one's job with one's qualifications and passion can transform a life that once appeared idle into one of excellence.

A Time for Courage, Not Just Conformity

The campus phase is when the seeds of courage must be sown—courage to think differently, to take a less-traveled path, to define your own success. This is the right time to make mistakes, to learn, to realign. What matters most is not how fast you choose, but **how consciously** you do it.

To the students, professionals, and dreamers reading this—remember:

You don't have to have it all figured out on Day One.

You just have to start with awareness, honesty, and the willingness to realign when needed.

Because careers aren't just built. They are **discovered, refined**, and **designed**—step by step.

And the best place to begin that journey is right here, during your campus years.

PART III

EARLY CAREER: GAINING DEPTH

Audience: Freshers and Working Professionals (0–5 years)

You've graduated, you've crossed the first major milestone, and the applause has just settled. Welcome to the phase where real-world experience becomes your greatest teacher. The early career years—typically the first 0 to 5 years after graduation—are the foundation for everything you build later. This is the phase where your ideals are tested by reality, where your learning accelerates, and where the choices you make will shape your work ethic, attitude, and professional trajectory for years to come.

If Part II was about exploration and aligning yourself to your purpose, **Part III is about grounding yourself**. Here, depth matters more than breadth. It's not just about where you work, but how deeply you learn, how responsibly you show up, and how seriously you take your personal and professional growth.

CHAPTER 10

First Jobs – Taking the Right Jump

The moment you receive your graduation certificate, a new pressure begins—the pressure to get a job. For some, job offers may be in hand already. For others, the search has just begun. But irrespective of how early or late the opportunity comes, **what you choose in your first job matters deeply**. This is the point where your academic life ends and your professional identity begins to form.

This chapter aims to help you approach your first job with **clarity and awareness**, so you can build a meaningful and strong career path right from Day 1.

1. Choosing Experience Over Salary – The Long-Term View

The Temptation of the Paycheck

It's only natural to be excited about your first salary. After years of depending on your family, that first paycheck feels like freedom. But what happens when you choose a job just because it pays slightly more—even if it's in a completely unrelated field to your passion or strength?

Let's take an example.

Example: Meera, a Computer Science graduate, got two offers:

- One from a startup offering ₹5.5 LPA for a coding role with hands-on exposure to product development.
- Another from a customer support BPO offering ₹6.2 LPA with rotational night shifts and no technical learning.

Meera took the BPO job because of the better pay. Two years later, she felt stuck—no tech skills, no learning curve, and now competing with freshers for entry-level tech jobs.

What did she really earn in two years? Money—but not momentum.

What Experience Offers That Money Cannot

- **Exposure to Business Realities**: In a learning-rich role, you see how real problems are solved.
- **Hands-On Learning**: You get to do things—fail, retry, and improve.
- **Mentorship & Feedback**: You grow when you have a manager or team that corrects and guides you.
- **Clarity**: Only experience can teach you whether you truly enjoy the field you've entered.

In my own journey, I chose to go with the flow and took a field sales job. It wasn't glamorous, it didn't pay the highest, but it gave me a 360-degree understanding of customer behavior, business pressure, and street-smartness. I didn't realize it then, but it laid the foundation for my success in collections, risk, and eventually digital transformation leadership.

Lesson: **Don't chase the highest salary. Chase the highest learning potential.** The income will follow your impact.

2. Skill-Building vs. Profile-Building – Substance vs. Surface

The Illusion of a Fancy Profile

Let's look at two young professionals:

- **Arjun** joined a top consulting firm, but worked only on internal documentation. He had the brand, but not the experience.
- **Sonal** joined a small analytics startup. She had no brand name on her CV, but was managing client dashboards within six months.

Five years later:

- Arjun is still struggling to prove he can handle client responsibility.
- Sonal is a team lead in another firm, with strong skills and a reputation for delivery.

Moral: A good profile may get you noticed. A good skill set will keep you relevant.

What Does Skill-Building Look Like?

- Learning how to **analyze a problem** and provide a solution
- Gaining **functional knowledge**—how credit appraisal works, how digital onboarding happens, etc.
- Becoming proficient in **tools and technology** relevant to your field (e.g., SQL for analytics, Excel for operations, CRM for sales)
- Learning **stakeholder communication**—how to speak with customers, internal teams, and leadership

One of the best early professionals I mentored was a commerce graduate who joined the operations team of a lending firm. She spent her first year mastering loan disbursement systems, understanding policy gaps, and improving TATs. Today, she leads the entire ops unit—not because of her degree, but because of her **deliberate skill-building**.

3. The Value of Stability and Accountability – Staying Power Builds You

Why People Job-Hop Early

Many young professionals move jobs every 10–15 months. Some reasons:

- Slightly better salary
- Frustration with work
- Impatience with slow growth
- Peer pressure ("everyone is switching!")

But here's the trap: **Short-term gain often equals long-term pain.** Employers notice patterns. They question reliability. Most importantly, frequent jumps mean you never stay long enough to:

- Take responsibility for results
- See the outcome of your efforts
- Learn from your mistakes

Example: In my early career, I stayed longer in challenging roles—sales, collections, and credit—where pressure was high and targets were tight. But those tough months taught me perseverance, empathy, and business logic. When leadership roles opened up, I was ready—because I had built **depth**, not just a decorated CV.

Accountability: The Missing Ingredient in Many Early Careers

Taking ownership means:

- Showing up even when it's tough
- Taking responsibility for mistakes
- Going beyond your job description
- Saying, "This is on me," rather than blaming others

Freshers who learn accountability early often grow 2x faster than their peers. Why? Because trust is the real currency in any organization.

4. Realistic Examples – From My Observations

Let's revisit some of the stories shared in earlier chapters with a new lens:

- **Gopinath**, who pursued his passion in speech and writing, patiently waited for the right media opportunity. Had he joined a bank just to earn early, he might never have become a popular

TV anchor. **Lesson**: He followed skill + passion and waited for the right jump.

- **Bala**, who always dreamed of being a doctor, stayed the course. He built depth in one direction. That early clarity gave him lasting career satisfaction.
- **Pranav**, an Aeronautical Engineer, now works in digital banking. A brilliant mind, but the job doesn't use his core education. Perhaps, had he taken a little more time after graduation, he may have aligned better and felt more fulfilled.

Takeaway: Every decision in your early career is a **compound interest investment**. Either you compound your learning—or you multiply your regret.

5. Instant Gratification vs. Purposeful Growth

Often, we fall into the trap of wanting **results immediately**—a good job, high salary, quick promotion. But building a career is like planting a tree:

- You dig the soil (education)
- You plant the seed (first job)
- You water it daily (consistency)
- And only then do you see fruits (growth, salary, impact)

In the Tamil movie *Velaiyilla Pattadhari (VIP)*, the hero Raghuvaran faces this exact dilemma. Though he's an engineering graduate, he rejects irrelevant jobs and waits for the right one. Family pressures rise, friends get ahead, but he stays focused. Eventually, when he gets the right civil engineering job, he excels—proving that **right timing + right alignment beats hasty decisions.**

Moral: Be patient. Be strategic. Be loyal to your purpose, not your pressure.

6. Guiding Principles to Choose the Right Career Path After College

To choose wisely, ask yourself:

Guiding Question	What It Reveals
What subjects or activities excite me deeply?	Your **passion zone**
What comes naturally to me?	Your **strengths**
What kind of impact do I want to make in the world?	Your **purpose**
What do I want to learn for the next 2–3 years?	Your **learning focus**
Will this job help me grow in my chosen direction?	Your **career alignment**

What You Lose If You Don't Choose Wisely

- Wasted time in irrelevant jobs
- Frustration and burnout
- Constant career switches
- Lack of identity and confidence
- Delayed success

Remember: **You can course-correct later, but it's much harder than starting right.**

Final Thoughts – Make the First Jump Count

The first few years of your career are your **launch window**. They are not about fame, comfort, or big salaries. They are about building your foundation with:

- Learning
- Responsibility

- Resilience
- Clarity

Make your early choices consciously. Choose a path where your **potential is nurtured**, your **skills are sharpened**, and your **values are respected**.

Don't just take a job—start a journey.

Jump, but jump with awareness.

CHAPTER 11

The Importance of Cross-Functional Experience

As you settle into your career, one of the best gifts you can give yourself is cross-functional exposure. Many people hesitate to switch roles within their company or relocate for a new opportunity—but these decisions are often the very turning points that accelerate your growth.

1. Embrace New Roles – By Choice or By Order

Sometimes, your manager or organization may assign you to a different department—Sales to Collections, Credit to Strategy, or vice versa. Instead of resisting, embrace it. Each department is a new classroom.

In my journey, I've worked across Sales, Credit, Collections, and Strategy. Every role taught me something unique:

- **Sales** honed my persuasion and people skills.
- **Credit** taught me analytical and decision-making abilities.
- **Collections** trained me to handle pressure and build resilience.
- **Strategy** enabled me to think big-picture and drive transformation.

Each shift prepared me for future leadership. Without those transitions, I wouldn't be where I am today.

2. Be Flexible with Location – Growth Has No PinCode

Early in your career, mobility is your strength. Say yes to transfers, regional roles, or even tough geographies. Working in new regions enhances your adaptability, cultural awareness, and problem-solving ability.

Example:

- A friend moved from Chennai to a small town in Madhya Pradesh for a collections role. Two years later, he was promoted ahead of his batch because of his performance in a challenging location.

Growth often hides in uncomfortable places. Be willing to go there.

3. Lateral Learning – Grow Across, Not Just Up

Career growth isn't just about vertical promotions. Lateral movements help you:

- Understand how departments connect
- Develop multi-dimensional problem-solving
- Build empathy for other teams' challenges
- Become a better collaborator and future leader

How to Navigate Internally for Cross-Functional Roles

- **Show Interest**: Tell your manager you're open to new challenges.
- **Build Trust**: Deliver results in your current role first.
- **Stay Curious**: Learn about what other departments do.
- **Volunteer**: Take part in cross-functional projects, task forces, or pilots.

Example:

- One of my colleagues in Credit spent time understanding how Risk models were built. Later, she transitioned into the Risk Analytics team and grew faster than others.

4. Final Thoughts – Don't Box Yourself In

Early career is your sandbox. Try new things. Fall. Learn. Repeat. When you take on diverse roles early, you:

- Build agility
- Discover hidden strengths
- Develop a broad lens to view business

Don't resist rotation. Seek it. That's how well-rounded professionals—and future leaders—are born.

CHAPTER 12

Choosing to Upskill, Choosing to Rise

One of the most underestimated superpowers in your early career is your willingness to learn continuously. If your first job is the platform, and cross-functional exposure is your breadth, then upskilling is your *depth*. This chapter is a call to action: to invest in yourself—not just through on-the-job learning, but through structured education, certifications, and personal discipline. It is a decision that distinguishes professionals who stagnate from those who evolve into impactful leaders.

1. Why Certifications and Courses Matter

The moment you step into a job, your academic degrees slowly start becoming historical data. What will keep you relevant in the long run is your ability to stay current, upgrade your tools, and deepen your value.

Certifications as Career Accelerators

- In technology, certifications in data analytics, cloud infrastructure, Python, or AI can unlock new-age roles.
- In BFSI, certifications like NISM, IRDA, Credit Risk, Treasury Management, or Regulatory Compliance fast-track growth.
- For managers and aspiring leaders, project management (PMP), Six Sigma, or leadership courses create structured thinking.

Example: A young professional in a Collections role took a Six Sigma certification. He used that knowledge to introduce process improvement frameworks and was soon promoted to a regional role handling analytics and operations.

Certifications act as proof of intent. They signal seriousness and commitment to growth. They differentiate a candidate in a pool of resumes.

2. The Power of Second Degrees and Part-Time Learning

Sometimes, your first degree may not represent your future goals. A second degree or part-time qualification bridges the gap between where you are and where you aspire to be.

Example: A B.Sc. graduate working at a rural loan branch pursued a part-time MBA in Finance. Through weekend classes and night studies, he built confidence and domain knowledge. Two years later, he transitioned into a zonal credit role with greater influence and visibility.

The Master CIO Journey – A Personal Reflection

When I enrolled in the Master CIO certification at Carnegie Mellon University, I was already well into my professional journey. Many questioned the need for it, especially at that stage of my career. But for me, it was nothing short of transformational.

- It wasn't just a technical program—it was a holistic leadership development journey.
- It challenged my thinking, broadened my horizons, and redefined how I saw IT as an enabler for business.
- It introduced me to global best practices, strategic frameworks, and world-class faculty who reshaped my approach to digital transformation.

What changed after that program wasn't just my resume—it was my mindset. I began seeing myself not as someone delivering IT projects, but as someone who could lead technology-led business transformation.

Lesson: Never underestimate the power of structured learning. In a world of noise and distractions, formal education provides clarity and direction.

3. When to Switch vs. When to Deepen Expertise

In the early career stage, there's always the temptation to keep switching—roles, companies, even domains. And sometimes, that's necessary. But wisdom lies in knowing when to jump and when to dig deep.

Switch When:

- You're completely disconnected from your job or industry
- You've hit a plateau and there's no opportunity for growth or skill enhancement
- You're stuck in a toxic or unchallenging environment that's eroding your motivation

Stay and Deepen When:

- You've found a domain that sparks your curiosity and passion
- You're working with leaders who support your growth
- You're given increasing responsibility and ownership of projects

Example: I once mentored a young analyst who got a tempting offer from a larger company with a higher salary. However, in his current role, he was leading two automation projects that had the potential to become game-changers. I advised him to stay and finish what he started. Today, he leads the automation vertical of a full business unit.

Switching gives you variety. Staying gives you legacy and expertise. True impact often comes from mastering a domain deeply over time.

4. Building a Learning Identity

You don't need a university or an employer to upskill. The best learners are self-driven. The internet offers everything—from YouTube tutorials to podcasts, from online academies to global webinars.

- Learn Excel deeply if you're in operations or MIS.
- Read regulatory updates if you're in compliance or credit.
- Take product courses if you're in sales or marketing.
- Follow industry thought leaders on LinkedIn.

Create a habit: Learn for 30 minutes every day. Read, reflect, and apply. Over months, it will build thought leadership.

Share what you learn with your team or on professional forums. This not only builds personal brand but also forces you to internalize concepts.

5. Final Thoughts – You Are Your Best Investment

In the end, your most valuable asset is *you*. Organizations may change. Teams may restructure. Bosses may rotate. But your knowledge, mindset, and skills stay with you.

"Don't wait for your company to sponsor your growth. Own it. Fund it. Drive it."

Take evening courses. Watch masterclasses. Invest in good books. Attend weekend workshops. Sign up for certifications. Explore second degrees.

You don't need permission to learn. You only need the hunger to grow.

Because when you choose to upskill, you choose to rise—not just in title, but in potential, confidence, and value.

Conclusion – Depth Before Flight: Why Early Career is the Foundation

Your early career is not just a stepping stone; it is the *foundation* upon which your entire professional journey is built. Many young professionals rush through this phase, eager to move up the ladder quickly. But the truth is, speed without direction can lead you off-course. What matters more is *depth*—the kind that builds clarity, character, and capability.

Revisiting the Journey

In **Chapter 10**, we talked about taking the right first job—not just chasing salary but seeking experience. You learned that your early choices should be about exposure, responsibility, and learning curves. We emphasized that your first job is less about brand and more about bandwidth—the bandwidth to make mistakes, try new things, and shape your identity.

In **Chapter 11**, we explored the power of cross-functional experience. You saw how moving across Sales, Credit, Collections, or Strategy doesn't dilute your growth—it sharpens it. You understood that being open to new roles, geographies, and challenges is what makes a future leader. When you say "yes" to roles outside your comfort zone, you gather wisdom that no classroom can teach.

In **Chapter 12**, we dived into the power of *upskilling*. From certifications to second degrees, from night classes to leadership programs, we saw how real growth often requires personal investment. My own Master CIO journey wasn't just a credential—it was a lens changer. It taught me that structured learning can unlock inner potential, elevate your thinking, and place you ahead of the curve.

Together, these chapters were not random ideas—they are pillars of a conscious early-career strategy.

What This Part Was Really About

1. **It's about** Mindset Shift Early career is where you transition from being a student to being a professional. But the learning doesn't stop. In fact, it accelerates—through work, through challenges, and through deliberate learning. The mindset shift is realizing: *You are responsible for your own growth.*
2. **It's about** Saying Yes to Uncertainty Cross-functional moves, new locations, project rotations—they all bring discomfort. But they also bring *compound learning*. Every new team, manager,

domain, or region adds to your strategic lens. Those who embrace this become irreplaceable assets in the long term.

3. **It's about** Building Career Capital When you choose difficult roles, meaningful certifications, or long hours of part-time study, you're building *career capital*. This capital doesn't show up immediately on your payslip—but it reflects in how people trust you, what roles you're considered for, and how fast you're pulled into the room where decisions are made.

4. **It's about** Discipline Over Distractions The early years can be filled with distractions—job hops for higher pay, FOMO from peers, or impatience to rise fast. But those who stay consistent in learning, delivering, and building depth eventually *overtake* the fast starters.

The Compounding Power of Depth

In finance, we talk about compound interest. In careers, the equivalent is *compound knowledge*. When you stay long enough in a role to master it, and simultaneously stay curious to learn beyond it, you begin to see how everything connects—products, customers, processes, risks, and strategy. That's when you become truly valuable.

You don't rise just by changing titles. You rise by *adding value* that others cannot.

The deeper your understanding, the wider your influence. The wider your influence, the faster your growth.

What Should You Carry Forward?

- Always choose roles that challenge you, not just reward you.
- Be proud of cross-functional stints—they're your leadership gym.
- Upskill even when there's no immediate return. It *will* pay off.

- Move locations, switch teams, embrace the unknown—early career is the best time to do it.
- Create a personal learning path that is independent of your employer.

Your Next Decade is Built Here

Most people underestimate their first 5 years and overestimate what they can do in the next 5. But if you treat your early years as your growth engine—fuelled by learning, discomfort, ownership, and exploration—your trajectory will be different. Not just upward, but meaningful.

This is your runway. Use it to gain depth, not just momentum. Because those who invest early, rise exponentially.

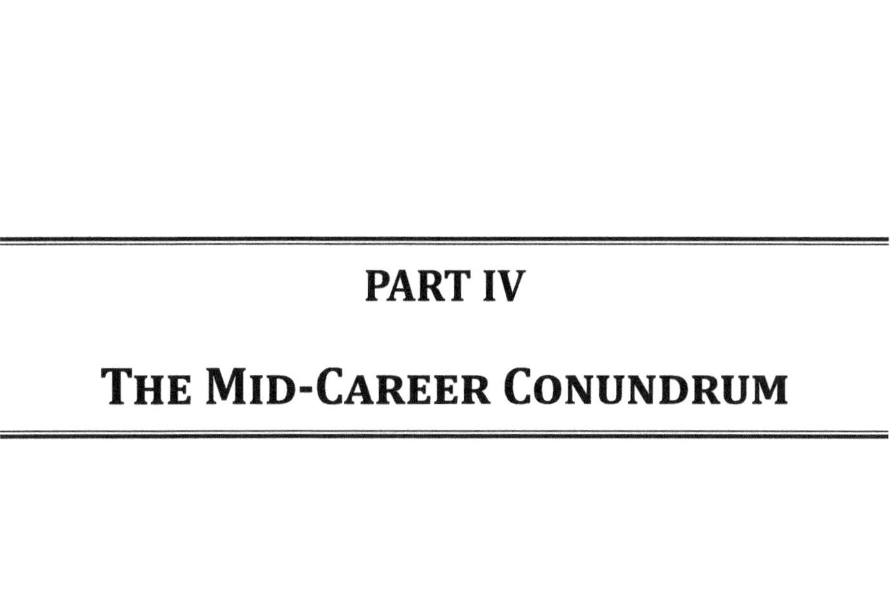

PART IV

THE MID-CAREER CONUNDRUM

Audience: Professionals (5–15 years experience)

The mid-career phase is perhaps the most misunderstood and underrated stretch in a professional's journey. You're no longer a fresher trying to prove yourself, but not yet at the top table making strategic decisions. It's a space where your experience becomes both an asset and a burden—where expectations rise, but clarity often doesn't. This is the time when performance reviews begin sounding repetitive, promotions start slowing down, and the inner voice grows louder: *"Am I stuck, or am I growing?"*

This section dives into that very tension—how to recognize when you've plateaued, when to dig deeper versus when to pivot, and how to start thinking like a leader even if your title doesn't say so yet. Whether you're feeling stuck in a role, trying to transition into leadership, or standing at a technology crossroad wondering what comes next, this part offers frameworks, real examples, and personal reflections to help you navigate this inflection point with clarity and confidence.

We begin with understanding the silent signs of stagnation in "Stuck in a Role? Or Growing in Place?", explore the mindset and skill shift required in "Transitioning to Leadership", and close with a real-world case study in "The Technology Crossroad", where strategic choices shaped the direction of an entire career—and business.

CHAPTER 13

Stuck in a Role? Or Growing in Place?

There comes a moment in every professional's life—often around the 8 to 12-year mark—when the excitement of early career jumps starts to fade, and a sense of stasis creeps in. You might be doing well by external metrics: stable job, decent income, steady promotions. Yet, inside, you begin to question: *Am I growing? Or am I just surviving?*

This chapter is about identifying that phase—not with fear or panic—but with clarity and purpose.

1. Recognizing Plateaus and Burnout

Plateau is when you've stopped learning, but you haven't yet acknowledged it.

Burnout is when you've stopped caring, and you haven't admitted it to yourself.

I've personally experienced both.

In one of my early leadership roles, after years of success in Collections and Credit, I began feeling that every day was a repetition of the last. I had processes on autopilot, a team that delivered, and a track record that was "comfortable." But that comfort was deceptive. I wasn't growing. I was coasting.

The real moment of truth came when I caught myself avoiding new initiatives—not because they were hard, but because they seemed like a distraction from my "stable rhythm." That's when I realized I was stuck in a silent plateau.

If you:

- Stop reading about your domain
- Stop seeking feedback
- Feel irritated by new challenges
- Avoid presentations, reviews, or visibility
- Secretly envy others who are growing

…you may be at a plateau or on the edge of burnout.

2. Internal Growth vs. External Movement

The immediate reaction to such stagnation is to jump—quit the job, find another one, reset.

But is external movement always the answer? Not necessarily.

Sometimes, the biggest breakthroughs happen internally—within the same organization or role—if we actively seek growth.

Internal Growth Opportunities:

- Move to another function (e.g., I transitioned from Credit to Strategy)
- Lead a special project or digital transformation (like my shift to heading Business Solutions and IT)
- Ask to mentor junior teams or onboard new recruits
- Volunteer for cross-location or cross-BU responsibilities

These don't change your title overnight—but they expand your skills, network, and narrative.

I remember during my time at Tata Motors Finance, I was already managing high-value portfolios. But the real growth came when I was entrusted with building digital IPs in the Collections space. It was a challenge *within* the system—but one that gave me new energy and purpose.

That said, sometimes the organization may have hit its own plateau in terms of what it can offer *you*. That's when **external movement** becomes necessary—not as an escape, but as evolution.

Ask yourself:

- Are my contributions being recognized meaningfully?
- Am I being challenged intellectually?
- Are the next 2 years going to be more of the same?

If the answers are consistently "no," you might need to take a bold step.

3. Talk to Mentors, Not Just Managers

Managers are transactional. Mentors are transformational.

Managers focus on your current deliverables. Mentors focus on your long-term potential.

In my journey, I've been fortunate to have mentors like Mr. Arun Diaz—someone who, as a board member, went beyond organizational conversations and invested in *me* as a person. His guidance during periods of internal churn gave me clarity on what really mattered: legacy over hierarchy, meaning over motion.

Make it a habit to cultivate at least 2–3 mentors who:

- Are outside your direct reporting chain
- Are from different industries or geographies
- Have no stake in your current success, only in your long-term growth

Mentors will ask you questions managers don't:

- "Are you fulfilled?"
- "Where do you want to be 10 years from now?"
- "What are you doing today that your future self will thank you for?"

And most importantly, mentors help you *see yourself clearly*. That alone can be the trigger you need to break out of inertia.

4. Building a Mid-Career Compass

Here are some self-check questions to ask at this stage:

1. **Impact**: Am I adding real value, or just ticking boxes?
2. **Learning**: When was the last time I learned something new at work?
3. **Energy**: Do I look forward to Monday mornings?
4. **Visibility**: Are my contributions known and recognized beyond my immediate team?
5. **Legacy**: What will I be remembered for if I leave tomorrow?

If your answers concern you, don't panic. Get curious. Get moving. Growth is always possible—but only if you recognize the stillness first.

Final Thoughts

Stagnation is not a crime. Staying stuck knowingly is.

Mid-career is not a dead-end. It's the launchpad for reinvention—if you're willing to ask hard questions and seek new answers. Don't fall into the trap of comfort. Comfort is not the same as growth.

> *"Don't wait for your role to grow you. Grow yourself, so that your role evolves with you—or makes way for your next one."*

Your best years may still be ahead of you—but only if you make space for them.

Chapter 14

Transitioning to Leadership

The biggest shift in a professional's life doesn't come from a title change. It comes from a mindset shift—from being a doer to becoming an enabler, from focusing on tasks to building direction, from personal delivery to team success. This chapter is about making that leap—consciously, strategically, and courageously.

1. Thinking Beyond Your KRAs

For most of our early and mid-career, our world revolves around KRAs (Key Result Areas). We are conditioned to think in terms of performance metrics, targets, and deadlines. But leadership begins when you stop limiting yourself to what is *assigned* to you and start taking ownership of what needs to be *achieved*.

I remember an assignment where I was overseeing Collections. My KRA was to ensure recovery targets were met. But I realized there was a deeper opportunity: customers were dropping into delinquency due to poor onboarding and unrealistic repayment expectations. I collaborated with the Credit and Sales teams to propose a pre-disbursal engagement protocol. This wasn't my KRA. But it reduced the bounce rate significantly. It also earned me visibility as someone who thinks end-to-end—not just within my boundaries.

Leadership begins when you start asking: "What is the outcome we want to achieve?" and not just "What is my task?"

2. From Execution to Strategy

Execution is about getting things done. Strategy is about knowing what should be done—and why. The mid-career phase demands this switch. While execution makes you reliable, strategic thinking makes you valuable.

I experienced this during a transformation project involving CRM and LOS systems. Initially, I was involved in defining business requirements. But soon I realized that unless we redefined how different departments interacted, any tool we built would fail. I stepped back, studied interdepartmental handoffs, mapped friction points, and brought the heads of departments into design workshops. This was not part of my original mandate—but it was what the *project* needed.

That experience taught me that leaders don't just accept deliverables—they shape them. They question assumptions, connect dots, and think of second- and third-order impact.

3. Building Teams, Not Just Completing Tasks

One of the most transformational realizations in leadership is that your real output is no longer what *you* do, but what your *team* achieves. This is where many mid-career professionals struggle. They were great individual contributors. But they find it hard to let go of control.

In one of my roles, I was leading a cross-functional team tasked with improving digital loan disbursements. We had product owners, developers, testers, and operations folks. Initially, I used to check every document, approve every wireframe, attend every test case demo. It was exhausting—and unsustainable. One of my mentors advised: "Empower. Don't micromanage."

I shifted focus to coaching the team leads, defining clear expectations, and building trust. Not only did the delivery improve, but the team also grew in confidence. Some of them went on to lead their own verticals.

Lesson: Leadership is not about knowing everything. It's about creating an environment where others can bring their best.

4. Owning the Culture and Narrative

Mid-career leaders often underestimate their influence. Whether you realize it or not, people are watching you. How you respond to stress. How you speak about your seniors. How you treat peers and juniors. You are shaping culture every single day.

In one of my roles, there was significant resistance to a new digital initiative. Instead of pushing harder, I began having open forums, weekly learning sessions, and invited skeptics to co-lead pilots. The narrative slowly changed—from fear of change to curiosity about what's possible.

The shift to leadership is also the shift to storytelling—of being the voice that inspires confidence, not just gives instructions.

5. Final Thoughts – The Internal Promotion That Matters Most

You may or may not get promoted right away. But the transition to leadership is an *internal* promotion. It's the decision to behave, think, and deliver like someone who holds the bigger picture. It is the choice to rise, even before someone hands you the designation.

Don't wait for a title to start acting like a leader. Start acting like one, and the title will follow.

This transition is not always comfortable. But it is always worthwhile. Because the moment you choose to lead—not just perform—you open up a new horizon of impact, influence, and legacy.

CHAPTER 15

The Technology Crossroad – A Case Study

There comes a moment in many mid-career professionals' lives where a unique opportunity presents itself—one that isn't in your comfort zone but has the potential to transform your career. For me, that moment came after 16 years of rigorous experience in the business trenches—sales, collections, credit, and field strategy. I was given the chance to head the Centre of Excellence (CoE) and Strategy. What seemed like a functional shift turned out to be a career-defining inflection point.

Initially, I wasn't sure if I was the right person for the role. My expertise was rooted in customer behavior, operational nuances, and team management—not technology. But that was exactly why I succeeded. Because technology is never just about systems—it's about solving real business problems. My years in the field gave me the clarity to see pain points and inefficiencies that others often missed.

As I led Process Improvement and Digitization, I brought my business experience to the table. I wasn't building tech for the sake of innovation—I was enabling tools that could solve real problems in the field. I remember digitizing the collections strategy and onboarding journeys. The adoption rates were high, not because the tech was fancy, but because the solutions were rooted in the realities of our customer-facing teams.

1. Why Understanding Tech is Key in Any Domain

Whether you are in Sales, Risk, Legal, or Strategy—technology is not a support function anymore. It is the core enabler of scale, efficiency, and differentiation. If you don't understand how technology works, you will always be dependent on someone else to bring your ideas to life. Worse, you may never realize what's possible.

Understanding tech doesn't mean you have to code. It means understanding workflows, data points, system integrations, user journeys, and how to translate a business challenge into a tech requirement.

In one instance, we were struggling with TATs in the loan underwriting process. Many suggested increasing manpower. But with some analysis, we found that manual handoffs and data verification delays were the bottlenecks. We automated data pulls from bureau and GSTN sources and reduced TAT by 40%. That's the power of tech when driven by someone who understands both sides.

2. Bridging Business Needs with Tech Solutions

The most valuable people in any organization today are the ones who can bridge business and technology. They understand the "what" and the "why" from business—and can co-create the "how" with tech.

I have seen IT teams build dashboards that never get used, and business teams request changes that are impossible to implement. That gap exists when both sides don't speak each other's language.

My journey taught me that I didn't have to become a tech expert. I had to become a translator—a bridge. I started using tools like process maps, BRDs, and customer journey canvases. I ensured tech teams joined field visits. I made business teams attend UATs.

This simple shift of working as one team—rather than two silos—was transformative.

Lesson: If you want to be irreplaceable in your mid-career journey, become the bridge. Not everyone needs to be a techie. But everyone needs to be tech-aware.

Conclusion: Owning Your Mid-Career Narrative

The mid-career phase is often the most misunderstood—and most underestimated—segment of professional life. It is the phase where experience begins to solidify, but aspirations remain fluid. Where confidence builds, but questions also deepen. It is neither the hunger of early years nor the settled maturity of late career—it's the search for clarity amidst the climb.

In this part of the book, we navigated through some of the most defining questions that professionals encounter between the 5–15 year mark:

- **Am I growing or just moving?**
- **Am I leading or just delivering?**
- **Should I stay in my lane or explore new ones?**
- **Is it too late to learn something entirely new?**
- **What if I make a shift and fail?**

These are not just career questions. These are identity questions. And that's why the answers don't come from the market. They come from within—from a place of self-awareness, reflection, and courage.

In **Chapter 13**, we learned that getting "stuck" is not always a function of your job role. It can also be a sign of internal stagnation. The answer is not always to jump ship—it might be to re-energize your approach, reset expectations, or reconnect with your sense of purpose. And that begins by talking to **mentors**, not just managers. Managers manage your output. Mentors help you shape your outlook.

In **Chapter 14**, we crossed the invisible line from execution to leadership. Leadership isn't about control—it's about culture. It's about shaping outcomes, owning the narrative, and building a team that outgrows your individual capacity. It means thinking beyond your KRAs, embracing ambiguity, and asking better questions, not just seeking faster answers.

You would have read how I moved from meeting recovery targets to solving the root causes of delinquency, or how I let go of micromanagement to empower my team. Those weren't just managerial upgrades—they were mindset milestones.

And in **Chapter 15**, we walked together through my personal journey from field operations to technology leadership. That shift wasn't driven by a degree in coding. It was driven by a belief—that technology is only as useful as its understanding of real-world problems. My background in business became my biggest advantage in IT. I didn't speak "tech," but I spoke "value." And that made all the difference.

The deeper message of this chapter is not just about moving to IT. It's about recognizing and acting upon **your own crossroad**—whatever and wherever that may be. You don't need to have it all figured out. You just need the curiosity to explore, the humility to learn, and the courage to leap.

Mid-Career is Not the Plateau. It's the Pivot.

This part of your journey is not about ticking boxes or chasing promotions. It's about crafting your **narrative**. Choosing what kind of leader, learner, and legacy-builder you want to be. It's where you move from **doing work** to **designing impact**. Where you go from being known for your **skills** to being recognized for your **wisdom**.

Titles may or may not come. But transformation will—if you choose to show up, step up, and look up.

So pause. Reflect. And then realign. Because the most powerful chapters of your career are still ahead—and it is here, in the midst of this mid-career conundrum, that you begin to write them with intention.

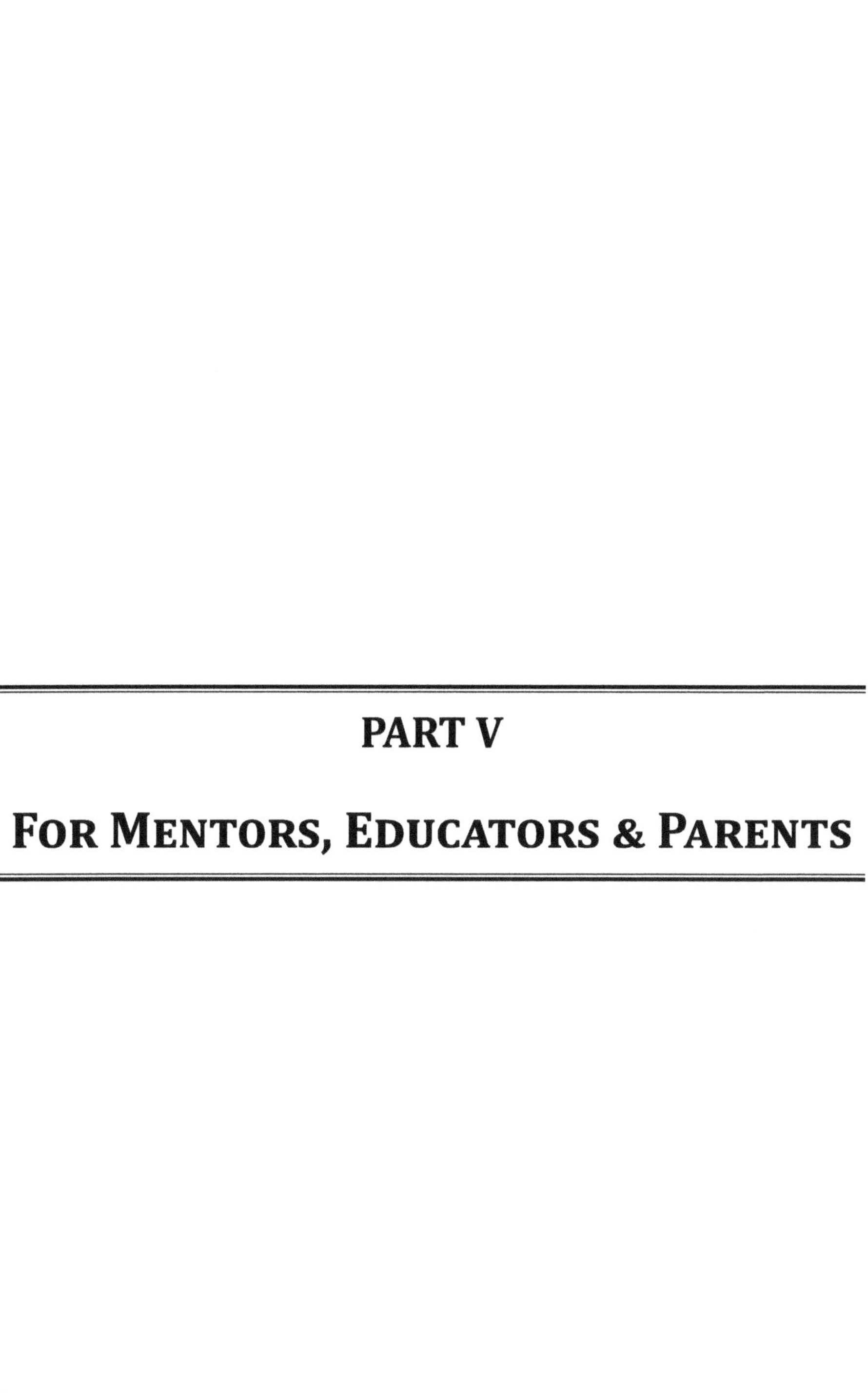

PART V

FOR MENTORS, EDUCATORS & PARENTS

Introduction

This part is dedicated to those who guide others—not by choosing for them, but by enabling them to choose wisely. Whether you are a parent nurturing a child's first spark of curiosity, a teacher shaping young minds, or a mentor guiding professionals through career crossroads, your role is sacred.

The impact of good mentorship is lifelong. A word of encouragement, a patient conversation, or a subtle nudge in the right direction can shift someone's path for the better. Yet, it's not just about giving advice. It's about *observing deeply*, *listening intentionally*, and *empowering without overpowering*.

In the chapters ahead, we explore how to become effective enablers of growth across all life stages—from a school-going child with untapped creativity, to a mid-career professional wondering if they missed their calling.

CHAPTER 16

The Art of Observing Potential

True mentorship doesn't begin with speaking. It begins with seeing.

We often think of potential as something to be developed—but the first step is to notice it. Every person, young or old, shows subtle signs of their inner inclinations. Some draw patterns, some ask "why" more often than "what," some naturally organize, while others imagine. Whether it's a ten-year-old assembling LEGO with stunning symmetry, a college student who volunteers to anchor every event, or a working professional who instinctively takes on people issues—these are not just habits; they are windows into *potential*.

1. How to Spot Early Inclinations

a) For Students (School Level):

- A child who rearranges things in order repeatedly may show early signs of analytical thinking or systems orientation.
- One who writes stories or questions everything might be leaning toward communication or research.
- The one who volunteers to lead the class, even in small games, might be a born organizer or leader.

Example: A 7th-grade student who constantly doodled in the margins was always scolded for not paying attention. But a teacher chose to observe instead of reprimand—and gave her a chance to design the classroom poster. Today, she is a UX Designer at a global tech company.

b) For College Students:

- Do they show consistency in certain types of projects? A marketing student always building case studies involving social causes might be drawn to development communication.
- Are they collaborative or independent workers? Do they naturally drift toward building networks or deep diving into research?

Example: One student I mentored used to take up backstage coordination roles in every college fest. Everyone thought he was shy, but what he was doing was managing operations. He now heads backend logistics for an e-commerce startup.

c) For Working Professionals:

- Not all career redirections are dramatic. Sometimes, a person's daily behavior gives you clues.
- Someone who enjoys building processes even in sales may have a natural fit for Product or Operations.
- A field executive who designs simple workarounds for repetitive issues may have a solutioning mindset ideal for Process Excellence or Digitization.

Example: In one of my earlier roles, a Collections Executive always documented his customer visits in a structured format. He wasn't asked to. He just enjoyed it. I brought him into a MIS and Quality Control role. He eventually moved into the Strategy Team.

2. Encouraging Without Imposing

This is where most mentors go wrong. Spotting potential doesn't mean pushing someone into a mold. It means creating an *environment* where that potential can bloom.

- Parents often try to "correct the course" when they feel a child's interest doesn't match societal or personal expectations.

- Teachers may guide a student toward where they excel, not where they are excited.
- Mentors might shape their mentees into their own image rather than helping them shape their own.

Example: A young engineer in my team was extremely good at documentation and product demos. His manager kept asking him to focus on coding. But when I spent time understanding him, I realized he was drawn to technical pre-sales. He moved to that function and flourished.

Encouragement is not direction—it is space, trust, and feedback. Give them opportunities, observe how they respond, and support their rhythm—not yours.

3. Building Character Over Competition

Success without grounding often leads to burnout or regret. A student may top the charts but feel directionless. A professional may win awards and still feel unfulfilled. Why? Because the focus was on outperforming others—not on becoming oneself.

Mentors must prioritize:

- **Integrity over achievement**
- **Curiosity over compliance**
- **Self-worth over external validation**

This becomes even more important today, where social media amplifies comparison and competition. Teach them to ask:

- *What do I enjoy doing, even if no one rewards me for it?*
- *What kind of work makes me feel alive—not just validated?*
- *What values will I not compromise on, even for success?*

Example: In a session with high-performing management trainees, I asked them to write down what they *wouldn't* do even for a promotion. Their answers revealed more about their real selves than any CV.

Character is the compass. Career is the vehicle. Without the compass, the vehicle only moves fast—but not necessarily in the right direction.

How Parents, Teachers & Mentors Can Enable Better Choices

Role	Enable by...
Parents	Listening more than advising. Encouraging exploration before setting expectations. Modeling balanced choices.
Teachers	Giving diverse exposure—not just syllabus-based. Noticing unique strengths in non-academic areas. Encouraging peer learning.
Career Counselors	Mixing aptitude tests with real conversations. Helping people *understand themselves*, not just pick a course. Staying updated with evolving fields.

Closing Thought for the Chapter

"The best mentors don't provide all the answers. They help others ask better questions."

Let us build a generation that knows how to look within before looking outside, and choose a path not because it is safe—but because it is *theirs*.

CHAPTER 17

Designing Ecosystems for Success

"It takes a village to raise a child—and a well-connected ecosystem to shape a career."

We often ask students: *What do you want to become?* But rarely ask: *What environment are we creating to help them become it?*

Career growth doesn't happen in silos. It's not just the job of parents or the responsibility of teachers. It's a collective effort—of schools, colleges, industry, government, and society at large. This chapter explores how we can create real, meaningful ecosystems that nurture potential, offer exposure, and empower decision-making—especially at the crucial school and college stages.

1. Role of Schools and Colleges in Career Mentoring

The foundation of career clarity starts early. Unfortunately, our current system often postpones it until it's too late—usually after results are out, or during last-minute college counseling.

How can schools help?

- Start career conversations by **Grade 8 or 9**—not as pressure points, but as explorations.
- Invite professionals from diverse careers—not just engineers, doctors, and IAS officers—to talk to students.
- Include a "Career Discovery Hour" monthly: a session where students learn about lesser-known but exciting careers (e.g., Wildlife Conservationist, UX Designer, Ethical Hacker, Behavioral Economist, Product Manager).

Example: In one of the schools I worked with, a quarterly "Career Café" event was introduced where parents and alumni spoke about their professional journeys. A Class 10 student, inspired by an alum who worked in Animation, later pursued a design degree—something he had never considered.

How can colleges amplify this?

- Every college should have a Career Enablement Cell—not just for placements, but for ongoing mentoring.
- Faculty advisors can be trained in basic career counseling techniques and industry understanding.
- Regularly track student interest and aptitude to help guide course selection, electives, and internships.

Example: During my own college years, the absence of structured mentoring often left us relying on peer advice or family opinion. Looking back, even a basic three-session mentorship program would've saved many from drifting into the wrong course or job.

2. Collaborating with Industry for Internships & Exposure

Real exposure changes everything.

One of the biggest gaps today is the lack of *real-world interface*. Students study theory but have no clue how it translates to actual work. This is where internships—when done right—become powerful tools for exploration, confidence, and clarity.

What makes internships meaningful?

- **Structured programs**: Clearly defined roles, mentors, and feedback loops.
- **Diversity of exposure**: Rotations across teams, shadowing seniors, or working on mini-projects.
- **Reflection and review**: Help students think about what they learned—not just what they did.

Example: At one of the organizations I worked in, we designed a summer internship for final-year students. Instead of assigning them to random tasks, we made them part of ongoing transformation projects. One intern, who worked on a Collections Dashboard, eventually joined us full-time and later became a key resource in the Business Analytics team.

For schools:

- Tie up with local businesses to offer short "industry visits" or 1-week observation internships.
- Allow students to present learnings to their classmates—it inspires curiosity and builds communication skills.

For colleges:

- Partner with industry for not just summer internships, but part-time semester-long projects.
- Invite industry mentors to run "Problem-Solving Labs" where students can bring in real business issues and brainstorm solutions.

Generic Example: A marketing student from a Tier 2 college worked on a real-time social media campaign for a local brand. He used the campaign as a portfolio to land his job—not his degree.

3. Making Career Fairs Meaningful

Career fairs often become brochure distribution events—where companies showcase themselves, and students collect freebies. To make them meaningful, we need a shift in purpose.

Transform Career Fairs into Career Conversations.

Key Ideas:

- Organize **theme-based zones**: Finance, Design, Technology, Social Impact, Entrepreneurship.
- Include **experience booths**: Try a mock trading session, a UX challenge, or a product pitch.

- Include **career mentoring pods**: Short 15-minute slots where students can talk 1-on-1 with professionals.
- Add **reflection zones**: After every session, students write down or discuss what they liked and what they didn't.

Example: In one institution, we replaced the annual placement fair with a "Career Discovery Day." No jobs were offered, but professionals across 25 domains engaged with students on real stories, failures, and decision-making. Feedback showed that 78% of attendees discovered new interest areas they had never considered.

4. The Role of Teachers, Parents, and Mentors in the Ecosystem

Everyone in the ecosystem has a role:

- **Teachers** should connect classroom learning with industry application.
- **Parents** must stay open-minded and help children explore beyond conventional careers.
- **Mentors** (including alumni) should volunteer time to offer real conversations, not just formal sessions.

Closing Thought

> *"A career is not chosen in isolation. It is nurtured in an environment of exploration, trust, and exposure."*

Designing such ecosystems doesn't require massive reforms—it starts with intention. One teacher deciding to invite a guest speaker. One college initiating a hands-on industry project. One parent encouraging their child to shadow a relative at work.

The ecosystem begins with us.

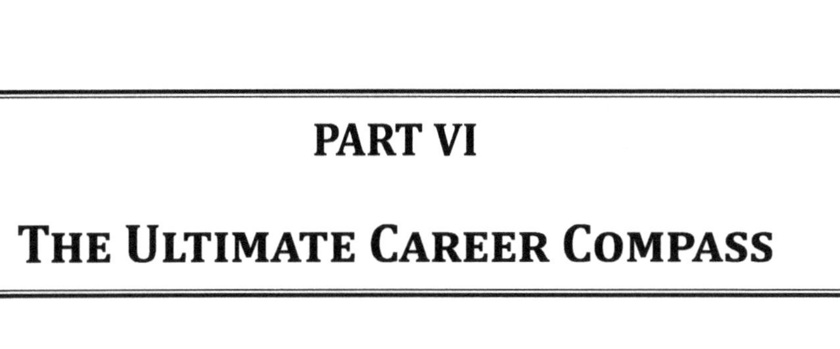

PART VI

THE ULTIMATE CAREER COMPASS

"Clarity is the foundation of choice. And choice is the beginning of change."

This final part of the book is for *everyone*—students standing at the edge of big decisions, professionals feeling stuck or restless, parents wanting to guide without bias, and mentors striving to support growth without imposition.

If the earlier parts were about understanding systems, psychology, and responsibilities, **this part is about building a personal compass**—one that helps anyone, at any stage, make aligned, confident career decisions.

There is no *one-size-fits-all* career answer—but there is a way to think clearly, evaluate thoughtfully, and move purposefully. This section will offer tools, models, and real-world stories that act as a compass—not to point to one fixed direction, but to help navigate any direction with confidence.

CHAPTER 18

The Framework to Make Better Life Decisions

Introduction

Why do some people make career choices that seem effortless—and others seem to struggle for years?

Often, it isn't intelligence or opportunity that makes the difference. It's *clarity of thought* and *structure in decision-making*. In this chapter, we introduce a simple but powerful framework that combines **self-awareness**, **market reality**, and **value-based reflection**—all of which are critical to make better life and career choices.

Section 1: A Step-by-Step Model to Evaluate Options

We often jump into decisions based on excitement, pressure, or herd mentality. Instead, this model encourages *conscious evaluation*.

The 6-Step Career Evaluation Model

1. **Define the Decision Clearly**

   o   Are you choosing a stream? A job switch? A role upgrade? A career break?

   o   *Clarity on the question leads to clarity in answers.*

2. **Understand the 'Why'**

   o   Is it for growth? Peace of mind? Prestige? Family expectations?

   o   Journaling this "why" often reveals unconscious motivations.

3. **List All Available Options**

   - Include even the "crazy ones" or less-traveled paths. Creativity starts here.

4. **Apply the 4-Quadrant Filter** *(explained below)*

5. **Speak to 2 People Who've Lived That Life**

   - Insights from people who've "been there, done that" will give practical reality.

6. **Revisit Your Own Values**

   - What matters most to you—freedom, purpose, challenge, income? Choose accordingly.

Tip: Don't rush this process. Sit with it. Reflect. Reassess. Decision-making isn't a race.

Section 2: The 4 Quadrants – Passion, Aptitude, Value, Demand

This is the heart of the chapter—a grid that helps evaluate any career choice or life path through **four essential filters**:

1. **Passion – Do I enjoy it?**

   - Would I do this even if I weren't paid?
   - Does it energize me or drain me?

Passion gives you fuel, but it needs the right engine to move.

2. **Aptitude – Am I good at it?**

   - Have I shown natural strength or quick learning in this area?
   - Do mentors or teachers affirm this skill?

Aptitude gives you edge and confidence. It makes growth sustainable.

3. **Value – Does it align with who I am?**

- Does this path resonate with my personal values (freedom, service, challenge, etc.)?
- Can I respect myself in this journey?

Without value alignment, even success can feel empty.

4. **Demand – Is there a market for it?**

- Will the world pay for this skill?
- Can I build a living or livelihood around this?

Passion without demand is a hobby. Demand without passion is a chore.

Real-World Application: The Career Quadrant Grid

Career Option	Passion	Aptitude	Value	Demand
Data Analyst	✓	✓	⚠	✓
Wildlife Photographer	✓	⚠	✓	⚠
Product Manager	⚠	✓	✓	✓
Teaching	✓	✓	✓	✓
HR in Corporate	⚠	✓	⚠	✓

Grey Zones = Areas to reflect further or develop through skilling/mentoring.

Section 3: Case Studies from Real-Life Professionals (From My Experience)

Case 1: Rekha – The Passionate Banker Who Chose Counseling

Rekha worked in banking for 12 years. She was high-performing but deeply unfulfilled. Her passion was people—listening, guiding, mentoring. I met her during a training program, and after several mentoring sessions, she applied the 4-Quadrant model.

- Passion ☑ : She loved mentoring.
- Aptitude ☑ : She was a natural listener.
- Value ☑ : It aligned with her need to make an impact.
- Demand ☑ : Counseling and coaching was growing fast.

She pursued a certification, started with weekend sessions, and today runs a full-time coaching practice—earning well and living her values.

Case 2: Raj – The Engineer Who Moved into Product Strategy

Raj was stuck in a technical role despite a deep interest in product design and customer behavior. During a digital transformation initiative I was leading, I saw his sharp thinking in problem-solving workshops and suggested he try a short Product Management course.

Using the quadrant:

- Passion ☑ (he loved strategy)
- Aptitude ☑ (fast learner)
- Value ⚠ (he wanted autonomy; initial roles were more structured)
- Demand ☑

He transitioned successfully within the organization after six months and is now a key member in the business solutions team.

Case 3: My Own Journey – From Strategy to Technology to Leadership

Coming from a business strategy and collections background, my own path into IT and Digital Transformation wasn't linear. But I followed this exact framework—what energized me, where I had strength, what mattered to me (impact and innovation), and whether the world needed it. That path led to CIO roles and transformation leadership. This model works because it's not about "perfect answers," but about *conscious alignment.*

Closing Thought

When you feel lost, don't look for a map—build a compass.

This chapter doesn't give you a formula—but it gives you something more powerful: a *filter to trust your own thinking*. With this framework, every crossroad becomes a conscious decision, not a desperate one.

CHAPTER 19

Future-Proofing Your Career

"The best way to predict the future is to build skills that grow with it."

In a world where technologies evolve by the quarter, industries pivot without notice, and job descriptions become obsolete in a few years, **future-proofing your career is no longer optional—it's survival**. But this isn't just about learning to code or mastering AI. It's about **agility of the mind, adaptability of the heart, and alignment with the world around us**.

In this chapter, we will explore how to stay relevant, confident, and resilient, even when the future is uncertain.

Section 1: Adapting in a Tech-First World

Gone are the days when only "tech folks" had to stay updated. Today, **every role—be it finance, sales, HR, or operations—demands digital fluency**.

Embrace Change, Don't Resist It

Early in my career, I was a part of core business roles—strategy, collections, field operations. But as technology became central to how we served customers and scaled businesses, I realized that **understanding digital tools and transformation was essential, not optional**. I made a conscious move from business to IT, not because I was a coder, but because I wanted to shape how tech could serve people better.

That shift—from fear of the unknown to curiosity about it—was the key.

"You don't have to be a techie. But you have to be tech-aware."

How to Build Tech Readiness (No Matter Your Role)

- **Subscribe to industry newsletters or YouTube explainers** (e.g., *TechCrunch, Harvard Tech Review*).
- **Experiment with low-code/no-code tools**: Automate small tasks.
- **Ask IT teams questions**: Be curious about what's coming in.
- **Join pilots or POCs**: Volunteer for testing new solutions.

Real Example: While implementing CRM and Voice Bot projects, I encountered team members who said, *"This is not my job, this is IT's domain."* The most successful ones? Those who asked questions, took ownership of UATs, and imagined how it could solve real pain points.

Section 2: Emotional Intelligence and Decision-Making

Technology may drive change, but it is **emotional intelligence (EQ)** that defines how we lead, collaborate, and evolve.

EQ > IQ in the Long Game

When I was leading transformation programs, I learned something crucial: **Projects don't fail due to bad technology; they fail due to bad communication, ego clashes, and lack of trust.**

Whether you are a manager or an entry-level professional, **your ability to listen, empathize, and collaborate** will keep you future-proof.

Develop Decision-Making with EQ

1. **Pause before reacting** – Tech speeds up execution; you need to slow down your *response.*
2. **Balance logic and empathy** – Understand what data says *and* how people feel.
3. **Include diverse voices** – Whether building a solution or choosing your next role.

From My Journey: In one of the key CRM projects, there was a moment when two functional leaders were at complete odds. It took active listening, repeated reframing of intentions, and emotional grounding to align the teams—not better tech.

"EQ is your lifelong OS—while tools and platforms are just apps."

Section 3: The Role of Networking, Mentors, and Continuous Learning

Networking is Not Just Events—It's Relationships

One of the most overlooked ways to future-proof your career is **staying in touch with people, not just platforms**. Many of my biggest career shifts—moving from business to IT, and from strategy to transformation—were made smoother by **mentors and networks** who backed me, guided me, or simply told me what I wasn't seeing.

Example: When I was transitioning into a digital leadership role, a former CIO mentor reminded me, *"Don't just learn the systems—learn how systems shape user behavior."* That changed the way I approached implementation and engagement.

How to Learn Continuously Without Burnout

- **Microlearning**: Read 10 minutes a day, not 2 hours once a week.
- **Courses that stretch, not stress**: Choose one course every 6 months. Make it stick.
- **Conferences & Webinars**: Attend one event quarterly—even if virtual.
- **Mentor others**: Teaching is the best form of learning.

Find (and Be) a Mentor

- **Reverse Mentoring**: Younger professionals can teach trends or tools; senior mentors offer perspective.

- **Be Open**: Mentorship doesn't always look formal. It might be a conversation after a meeting.
- **Give Back**: If you've learned something—share it. You don't need a title to mentor.

Future-Proofing Checklist

Area	Action
Tech	Follow one emerging trend (e.g., GenAI, No-Code)
EQ	Practice active listening in meetings
Learning	Pick one new skill or certificate every 6 months
Mentoring	Have one mentor; be one to someone else
Networking	Attend 2 meaningful events or connect with 5 professionals per quarter

Closing Thought

"Careers don't break because of big decisions. They drift because of small inactions."

To future-proof your career, you don't need to predict the next big thing. You need to stay adaptable, curious, emotionally intelligent, and well-connected. That's the real competitive edge. And it's available to *everyone.*

CHAPTER 20

The Fulfillment Factor

"Success may be measured in milestones. But fulfillment?
It's measured in meaning."

In a world obsessed with speed, salaries, and status, it's easy to forget why we started the journey in the first place. **We chase success, but rarely pause to ask: Is this what I truly want? Is this who I'm meant to be?**

This chapter isn't about climbing ladders. It's about building the right one—on a foundation of **purpose, values, and meaning**.

Section 1: Why Happiness Matters as Much as Success

From the outside, it often looks like those with high-paying jobs, corner offices, or impressive LinkedIn titles have "made it." But ask them privately, and you'll often hear words like: *"burnt out," "disconnected," or "trapped."*

I've seen professionals with excellent career graphs but deteriorating well-being, crumbling family ties, and a sense of emptiness that no promotion could fill. On the other hand, I've met people who may not have flashy careers—but they radiate joy, stability, and peace.

Lesson from Life: In my own career, there were moments when I was at the peak of delivery—managing transformations, working with leadership, getting recognized. But I also had nights where I questioned, *"Is this the life I'm designing, or is it just happening to me?"*

True career success is not just about "what you do" but **how it makes you feel**. When your work energizes you, not drains you—when you sleep peacefully, not anxiously—you know you're in the right space.

Signs You Have Success But Lack Fulfillment:

- You dread Mondays, despite high pay.
- You feel like you're always busy, but not progressing in *life*.
- You crave weekends and vacations not for rest, but for escape.
- You succeed at work, but feel a gap inside.

Section 2: Aligning Purpose with Profession

Many people believe purpose is some grand calling—something divine or rare. But more often, purpose is found in **doing what you're good at, for the right reasons, and in service of others**.

From My Journey: When I moved from business operations into digital transformation and IT, it wasn't just a career switch. It was a **shift in purpose**. I realized I could make a larger impact by shaping systems that helped *thousands* of employees and customers. I wasn't just solving business problems—I was solving *people problems* with tech.

How to Align Purpose and Profession:

1. **Identify your energy zones** – What tasks or roles make you feel most alive?
2. **Look at your impact** – Are you making lives better—customers, colleagues, family?
3. **Ask the "Why" behind your work** – If you removed the pay and perks, would you still feel proud of what you do?

Example:

A teacher doesn't just teach math—they shape thinking. A banker doesn't just process loans—they enable dreams. When professionals understand this layer, **purpose enters the picture**.

"Passion fuels you. But purpose focuses you."

Section 3: Legacy Thinking – What Will You Be Remembered For?

Success is often temporary. But **legacy is lasting**. At the end of your career, people may forget your job title or your CTC. But they'll remember:

- How you treated others.
- What you stood for.
- How you helped, mentored, or inspired them.

From My Life: One of the most fulfilling parts of my journey wasn't launching platforms or completing projects—but the messages I got from people I mentored or guided:

"Sir, your advice helped me choose the right role."

"You gave me confidence when I was about to quit."

These aren't KPI wins. They're **life impact moments**. They're what I'll carry with me far beyond retirement.

💬 **Questions for Legacy Thinking:**

- Who did I lift up along the way?
- Did I create systems that last, even in my absence?
- Will people remember me for my intelligence, or for my integrity?

"Legacy is not built in the last year of your career. It is built in how you show up every day."

The Fulfillment Factor Framework:

Element	What to Ask Yourself
Happiness	Am I joyful most days, or just productive?
Purpose	Do I know why I'm doing this work?
Alignment	Does my job reflect my values and strengths?
Impact	Who benefits from what I do—beyond me and my employer?
Legacy	If I left today, what would people say about me?

Closing Thought

"Careers may fill your bank account. Fulfillment fills your soul."

The real goal isn't to chase one and forget the other. It's to build a career where **success and happiness co-exist**, where your work reflects your inner compass, and where your journey becomes your legacy.

Because in the end, it's not about the role you held—but the *role you played* in the lives of others.

Conclusion – Part VI: The Ultimate Career Compass

As we come to the end of this part, it's time to reflect not just on career paths, but on the **life compass** that truly guides us.

Throughout this section, we've uncovered a powerful truth: **The best career decisions are not made in boardrooms, aptitude tests, or performance reviews—they're made in quiet, honest moments with oneself.** When we pause to align our choices with our passions, our natural abilities, our core values, and the demands of the world, we step into careers that don't just pay, but also *fulfill*.

We've seen how to build frameworks for life decisions, how to adapt in a tech-first world without losing the human touch, and how to keep fulfillment—not just success—at the heart of our pursuits.

In my own journey—spanning over two decades in business, strategy, IT, and transformation—I've experienced moments of clarity, confusion, breakthrough, and burnout. But at every critical juncture, the turning point came when I asked the deeper questions:

- *What truly drives me?*
- *Whose life does my work impact?*
- *Am I building a career, or am I building a life?*

These questions, though simple, have the power to reshape our journeys. I've seen colleagues reinvent themselves at 40, professionals restart at 50, and young students redefine success before 25. And all of them found direction when they **stopped looking for shortcuts and started listening to their inner compass**.

The Ultimate Career Compass is not a one-time tool—it is a lifelong mindset. It asks you to stay curious, stay humble, stay reflective. It asks you to upgrade your skills as much as your self-awareness. And above all, it invites you to measure success not just by how far you go, but by how aligned you remain with your values, joy, and purpose.

"Your career is not a race. It is a journey of discovery. And the only compass you need—lives within you."

So as you step into the next phase—whether you're choosing your first job, contemplating a switch, mentoring someone younger, or exploring a second innings—carry this compass with you. Let it guide your choices, shape your growth, and define your legacy.

This is more than a career path. This is your *life's work.*

CLOSING NOTE

As we come to the final pages of this journey, remember—*career choices are life choices*. They shape not just what you do, but who you become.

This book was written not as a textbook, but as a conversation—between me and you, between experience and aspiration, between confusion and clarity. I've walked this path—starting from modest academic roots, switching lanes multiple times, stepping into roles that seemed unfamiliar, and finally finding fulfillment in purpose-driven leadership. If there's one message I want you to take away, it's this:

You always have the power to choose again. To realign. To restart—not from scratch, but from experience.

Here's what I hope stays with you:

- **Clarity comes from exploration**—try, reflect, learn.
- **Potential must be nurtured, not dictated**—for students, professionals, and mentors alike.
- **Realignment isn't failure—it's evolution.** It takes courage to correct course.
- **A meaningful career lies at the intersection of Passion, Aptitude, Value, and Demand.**
- **The world is changing—so should your skills.** Adaptability and emotional intelligence are your greatest tools.
- **Mentors and networks matter.** Surround yourself with people who guide, not just instruct.
- **Fulfillment is as important as success.** Align your purpose with your profession.
- **Think long-term.** Your legacy is built through the choices you make every day.

Whether you're a student choosing your first path, a mid-career professional reevaluating your journey, a parent guiding your child, or a teacher shaping young minds—this book was for you.

In the end, it's not just about what career you choose. It's about *why* you chose it, *who* you became in the process, and *how* you used it to leave a mark on the world.

Here's to designing a career—and a life—that truly belongs to you.

With gratitude and purpose,
— **Vijay Vasudevan**

Sources & Acknowledgments

This book is a product of reflection, experience, and an earnest desire to guide individuals toward meaningful career decisions. While the thoughts and frameworks shared are rooted in my own professional journey, I stand on the shoulders of the timeless wisdom and generous insights that have shaped my understanding.

Classical Wisdom

Some concepts and slokas referenced in this book draw inspiration from **The Bhagavad Gita**, a spiritual and philosophical classic that continues to guide individuals in making righteous and purposeful life decisions. These references are widely accepted interpretations meant to provide contextual clarity and are in the public domain.

Personal Experiences

The narratives, examples, and reflections across this book are based on my own life—experiences as a student, a working professional, a leader, and a lifelong learner. I have taken care to avoid references to specific individuals or organizations unless in acknowledgment or with respectful anonymity.

Gratitude

A heartfelt thanks To Mr. Alok Chadha and Mr. Arun Diaz, for their invaluable guidance, encouragement, and unwavering belief in my journey. Your wisdom and mentorship have left a lasting impact on both my professional and personal life.

Guidance from Conversations

I also wish to acknowledge the thoughtful interactions with various educators, career counselors, and young professionals whose questions and challenges inspired much of what I've addressed in this book.

This book reflects my journey and learnings from 25 years in the banking industry. To ensure a smooth and polished reading experience, I have relied on tools like Copilot for creating images and ChatGPT for refining the language and enhancing sentence structure. While these tools have helped in presentation, the ideas, strategies, and experiences are entirely my own.

Every attempt has been made to ensure originality and authenticity. If any ideas resemble publicly available content, it is purely coincidental or used within the scope of fair and transformative use.